TO HEAVEN OR TO HELL

TO HEAVEN OR TO HELL

Bartolomé de Las Casas's *Confesionario*

David Thomas Orique, O.P.

The Pennsylvania State University Press
University Park, Pennsylvania

Library of Congress Cataloging-in-Publication Data

Names: Orique, David Thomas, O.P., 1959– author. |
    Casas, Bartolomé de las, 1484–1566. Aqui se con-
    tiené unos avisos y reglas para los confessores
    que oyeren confessiones delos Españoles que son o
    han sido en cargo a los Indios delas Indias del mar
    Oceano. English.
Title: To heaven or to hell : Bartolomé de las Casas's
    Confesionario/David Thomas Orique, O.P.
Other titles: Latin American originals.
Description: University Park, Pennsylvania :
    The Pennsylvania State University Press, [2018] |
    Series: Latin American originals | Includes biblio-
    graphical references and index.
Summary: "The first complete English translation and
    annotated study of Bartolomé de Las Casas's 1552
    Confesionario. Explores its history and its guide-
    lines for confessors administering the sacrament
    of confession to conquistadores, encomenderos,
    slaveholders, settlers, and others who had harmed
    indigenous peoples"—Provided by publisher.
Identifiers: LCCN 2017053085 | ISBN 9780271080987
    (pbk. : alk. paper)
Subjects: LCSH: Casas, Bartolomé de las, 1484–1566.
    Aqui se contiené unos avisos y reglas para los con-
    fessores que oyeren confessiones delos Españoles
    que son o han sido en cargo a los Indios delas Indias
    del mar Oceano. | Indians, Treatment of—Latin
    America—Early works to 1800. | Spain—Colo-
    nies—America—Early works to 1800. | Confes-
    sion—Early works to 1800.
Classification: LCC F1411.C33 O75 2018 |
    DDC 980/.00497—dc23
LC record available at https://lccn.loc.gov/2017053085

The Pennsylvania State University Press is a member
of the Association of University Presses.

It is the policy of The Pennsylvania State University
Press to use acid-free paper. Publications on uncoated
stock satisfy the minimum requirements of Ameri-
can National Standard for Information Sciences—
Permanence of Paper for Printed Library Material,
ANSI Z39.48-1992.

To all those who suffered and suffer
from conquests, then and now.

CONTENTS

Latin American Originals (LAO) is a series of primary-source texts on colonial Latin America. LAO volumes are accessible editions of texts translated into English—most of them for the very first time. Of the thirteen volumes now in print, nine illuminate aspects of the Spanish invasions in the Americas during the long century of 1494–1614, three push our understandings of the spiritual conquest into surprising new territories, and one—the present volume—is a bridge between both topics.

Taken in the chronological order of their primary texts, *Of Cannibals and Kings* (LAO 7) comes first. It presents the earliest written attempts to describe Native American cultures, offering striking insight into how the first Europeans in the Americas struggled from the very start to conceive a world that was new to them. *The Native Conquistador* (LAO 10) comes next, telling the story of the famous Spanish conquest expeditions into Mexico and Central America from 1519 to 1524—but through an indigenous perspective, built around an alternative leading protagonist (the ruler of Tetzcoco), written by his great-great-grandson. Viewed through the prism of the Ixtlilxochitl dynasty, the so-called conquest of Mexico looks startlingly different.

Next, chronologically, are LAOs 2, 1, and 9. *Invading Guatemala* shows how reading multiple accounts of conquest wars (in this case, Spanish, Nahua, and Maya versions of the Guatemalan conflict of the 1520s) can explode established narratives and suggest a more complex and revealing conquest story. *Invading Colombia* challenges us to view the difficult Spanish invasion of Colombia in the 1530s as more representative of conquest campaigns than the better-known assaults on the Aztec and Inca Empires. It complements *The Improbable Conquest*, which presents letters written between 1537 and 1556 by Spaniards struggling to found a colony along the hopefully named Río de la Plata. Their trials and tribulations make the persistence of the colonists seem improbable indeed.

Contesting Conquest adds intriguingly to that trio, offering new perspectives on Nueva Galicia's understudied early history. We read of the grim, messy tale of repeated efforts at conquest and colonization from the late 1520s through 1545, but from a surprising angle: our guides through those events are primarily indigenous witnesses and informants, their voices deftly identified, selected, and presented in LAO 12.

The History of the New World (LAO 11), slots in next, offering the first English translation since 1847 of significant portions of a 1565 Italian book that was a sixteenth-century best seller in five languages. Its author, the merchant-adventurer Girolamo Benzoni, mixed sharp observations and sympathy for indigenous peoples with imaginary tales and wild history, influencing generations of early modern readers and challenging modern readers to sort out fact from fable.

The Conquest on Trial (LAO 3) features a fictional indigenous embassy filing a complaint over the conquest in a court in Spain— the Court of Death. That text, the first theatrical examination of the conquest published in Spain, effectively condenses contemporary debates on colonization into one dramatic package. It contrasts well with *Defending the Conquest* (LAO 4), which presents a spirited, ill-humored, and polemic apologia for the Spanish Conquest, written in 1613 by a lesser-known veteran conquistador.

LAO volumes 5, 6, 8, and 13 all explore aspects of Spanish efforts to implant Christianity in the Americas. Chronologically, the present volume (LAO 13) comes first among these, as it presents the first complete English translation of a book by Bartolomé de Las Casas, originally published in 1552—not his famous *Very Brief Account of the Destruction of the Indies* but his *Confessionary for Confessors*. With its less compelling title and less sensationalist content, the *Confessionary* was before long overshadowed by the *Very Brief Account*, but at the time was just as controversial and—to conquistadors and many other Spaniards—outrageously offensive in its demand that Spaniards be denied confession and absolution until they publicly pledged to make restitution to the indigenous peoples they had abused and exploited. In LAO 13, then, we see an effort to make the conquistadors themselves subject to the spiritual conquest in the Americas.

Gods of the Andes (LAO 6) presents the first English edition of a 1594 manuscript describing Inca religion and the campaign to convert native Andeans. Its Jesuit author is surprisingly sympathetic to preconquest beliefs and practices, viewing them as preparing Andeans for the arrival of the faith from Spain. *Forgotten Franciscans* (LAO 5) casts new light on the spiritual conquest and the conflictive cultural world of the Inquisition in sixteenth-century Mexico. Both LAO 5 and 6 expose wildly divergent views within the church in Spanish America—both on native religions and on how to replace them with Christianity. Complementing those two volumes by revealing the indigenous side to the same process, *Translated Christianities* (LAO 8) presents religious texts translated from Nahuatl and Yucatec Maya. Designed to proselytize and ensure the piety of indigenous parishioners, these texts show how such efforts actually contributed to the development of local Christianities, leading to fascinatingly multifaceted outcomes.

The source texts in LAO volumes are colonial-era rare books or archival documents, written in European or Mesoamerican languages. LAO authors are historians, anthropologists, and scholars of literature who have developed a specialized knowledge that allows them to locate, translate, and present these texts in a way that contributes to scholars' understanding of the period, while also making them readable for students and nonspecialists. David Thomas Orique, O.P., himself a Dominican, has devoted his scholarly career to his Order's most celebrated friar, lending this series the benefit of his unique, specialized insight.

—Matthew Restall

ACKNOWLEDGMENTS

This book is a product of my years of studying the life, labor, and legacy of Bartolomé de Las Casas. In 1993, when I was a novice in the Order of the Friars Preachers, my interest in this narrowly understood and highly complicated Dominican friar began. I continue to seek to better understand his impact on the complex and conflictual history of the contact, conquest, and colonization of the American hemisphere—first by Spaniards and then by many others. These sixteenth-century themes confronted and contested by Las Casas continue to challenge and confound people in the twenty-first century.

While many have heard of or read English translations of Las Casas's well-known *Brevisima relación* (*Very Brief Account*) and are familiar with translations of other portions of his fourteen-volume corpus of writings in Spanish and Latin, more English translations of Las Casas's perspectives are needed. Accordingly, this first complete English translation of his *Confesionario* offers readers another treatment of the friar-bishop's sophisticated legal, theological, philosophical, historical, and anthropological views. This careful translation, its historical contextualization, and its analytic commentary provide readers with another sampling and example of the breadth and depth of Las Casas's vision for a more just world.

As with so many of life's efforts, debts of support are incurred. Gratitude is the currency to acknowledge this assistance. As such, I humbly recognize the assistance of others. I thank the many members of the Dominican community, at the local, provincial, interprovincial, and eternal levels, who have inspired and sustained my academic ministry. I also thank many other colleagues: at the University of Oregon, Professors Robert Haskett, Carlos Aguirre, Stephanie Wood, David Luebke, and Stephen Shoemaker; at Providence College, the students, staff, and faculty—especially in the History

Department—who offered resources and inspiration and provided examples that pushed me to complete this project. Special thanks go also to Sr. Dodi Poelzer, MM, for reading and commenting on manuscript drafts, as well as to Anne Marie Le Chevallier for her careful editing of the final text. And, of course, I also thank the wonderful people at Penn State—in particular Matthew Restall. All of you, in many ways, supported, modeled, and encouraged me as a scholar. Finally, I thank God, who with my parents gave me the gift of life and called me to a meaningful life of service.

This book offers the first complete and annotated English translation of Bartolomé de Las Casas's little-known 1552 publication of the
Confesionario para los confesores (Confessionary for confessors)—
also commonly referred to as *Avisos y reglas para los confesores
de españoles* (Advice and rules for confessors of Spaniards). In this
provocative theological treatise, which generated controversy akin
to that of his widely known legal tract—the *Brevísima relación de la
destruición de las Indias* (*Very Brief Account of the Destruction of
the Indies*), the Dominican bishop of Chiapa mandated a strikingly
innovative and allegedly harsh use of the Sacrament of Penance and
Reconciliation (that is, of confession) when confessors administer
this sacrament to conquistadors, *encomenderos*, slaveholders, settlers,
merchants, miners, ranchers, and any others who had maltreated or
profited from the indigenous people.[1] This groundbreaking sixteenth-
century treatise stipulated that confessors were required to ask these
Spaniards to make a secular and legal public pledge prior to or upon
entering the sacred and private reception of the sacrament, which
obligated them to restore what they had taken unjustly from the
indigenous people and to make restitution for the spiritual and physical harms done and for ill-gotten financial gains acquired. If these
penitents did not pledge to make restitution as specified, the confessor could not absolve these Spaniards' sins. Consequently, without
sacramental absolution, these Spaniards would remain in mortal sin.

1. *Encomenderos* were Spaniards who were given control over native populations by requiring the conquered to labor on and to pay tribute from their lands.

According to Catholic theological understanding of the time, dying in such an unabsolved state would bar them from eternal salvation and condemn them to the fires of hell.

While conforming to the dictates of the *Confesionario* would facilitate eternal salvation for the guilty Spaniards, its benefits for the indigenous peoples were both eternal and temporal. Early in his life, Las Casas maintained that the "primary and ultimate end" of the presence of the Spaniards in the Americas was the salvation of the native inhabitants and that their conversion required peaceful and persuasive evangelization, the method of catechizing that would result in their being baptized. Consequently, he condemned the wars against and the enslavement of the indigenous inhabitants because the unjust conquests and the exploitative colonization obstructed their evangelization and conversion, as well as deprived them of their lands and culture, of their sovereignty and freedom, and of life itself. In his struggle for temporal justice for the native peoples, Las Casas demanded publicly binding restitution as well as sacramental penance and absolution.

To better understand why and how Las Casas used the sacrament of confession as an ecclesiastical tool to achieve justice for the indigenous peoples, chapter 1 begins with Las Casas's own experience as a confessee, which in time revealed his own spiritual blindness, initiated his conversion of heart, and prompted his own act of restitution. Chapter 1 then presents how from 1514 to 1546 he explicated and promoted the doctrine and practice of restitution as a remedy for harms done.[2] Chapter 2 introduces the reader to Las Casas's bold use of the sacrament by presenting the genesis of the first *Confesionario* manuscript during 1546 and 1547. The chapter continues with the trajectory of events that shaped and generated his 1552 publication of an augmented *Confesionario* in a treatise titled *Aquí se contienen unos avisos y reglas para los confesores que oyeren confesiones de los españoles que son o han sido en cargo a los indios de las Indias del mar Océano, colegidas por el obispo de Chiapa don fray Bartolomé de Las Casas o Casaus, de la orden de Sancto Domingo.*[3]

---

2. Las Casas's utilization of the sacrament of confession is sometimes referred to as wielding an ecclesial weapon.

3. Las Casas, *Obras completas*, 10:267–388. This work is titled in English as "Here are contained some advice and rules for confessors who might hear the confessions of the Spaniards who are or have been in charge of the Indians of the Indies of

Chapter 3 offers an analytic commentary on the text of the *Confesionario* to elucidate general distinctive features of the treatise, as well as specific salient aspects of its *Argumento, Doce reglas,* and *Adición.* This chapter concludes with a brief synoptic discussion of the relationship of justice to restitution. These three introductory chapters are followed by the first complete English and annotated translation of the 1552 publication.

---

the sea Océano, compiled by the bishop of Chiapa, don friar Bartolomé de Las Casas or Casaus, of the Order of Saint Dominic." This treatise is also commonly referred to as *Avisos y reglas* and as the *Confesionario;* both titles are used in this book.

1

"I, Bartolomé de Las Casas or Causas . . .": An Encounter
with Temporal Justice's Rough Terrain

On the Caribbean island of Hispaniola, sometime between the Sun-
days of lighting the first Advent candle in 1511 and of celebrating
the flames of Pentecost in 1514, a young secular cleric, Bartolomé
de Las Casas, sought God's mercy and forgiveness in the Sacrament
of Penance and Reconciliation from one of the resident friars of the
Order of Preachers.[1] While kneeling in the confessional of a mod-
estly constructed church, Las Casas was shocked when the Dominican mendicant confessor refused him absolution because the young
Sevillian clergyman held indigenous peoples in *encomienda*.[2] Indeed,
in 1509, Adm. Diego Colón, Columbus's eldest son, who replaced
Nicolás de Ovando as governor of the Caribbean island, had given
land in Cibao and a *repartimiento* of Tainos to the young secular
priest; in 1513 deputy-governor Diego Velázquez also granted Padre

1. The first community of Dominican friars in America (the Indies) arrived in
1510 at the Spanish colonial city of Santo Domingo and consisted of three priests
(Pedro de Córdoba, Antón de Montesinos, and Bernardo de Santo Domingo) as well as
one lay brother (Domingo de Villamayor).
2. The *encomienda* was the earliest basis for coerced labor in the Spanish colonies and resulted in the widespread exploitation and mistreatment of the indigenous
population by the Spanish encomenderos. An encomienda was a grant of indigenous
laborers made to Spanish conquerors and settlers in Spanish America. The encomienda
grant conceded the right to tribute and free labor, as well as the obligations of military
service in times of emergency (there was no standing army until 1762) and support of
the church and priests for the instruction of the indigenous population. Lippy, Choquette, and Poole, *Christianity Comes*, 37; Adorno, *Polemics of Possession*, 11. Leddy
Phelan points out that the encomienda system was intended, at least ideologically,
to be a method of Christianizing the indigenous people. *Millennial Kingdom*, 83.

FIG. 1 The inland port on the Guadalquivir River in Bartolomé de Las Casas's birthplace of Seville became the gateway to the West Indies. Alonso Sánchez Coello, *Vista de Sevilla*, last quarter of the sixteenth century. Photograph: Wikimedia Commons.

Las Casas a repartimiento near Xagua in Cuba.[3] Although Las Casas considered himself a "good" encomendero and a man of peace, in the eyes of these Dominican friars, he was just like the rest.

While accompanying several military expeditions in Cuba, however, the gentleman-cleric saw the tragic massacres of indigenous people and observed their maltreatment on encomiendas, as well as witnessed the destruction of native life by the Spaniards' enslavement of the indigenous workers for gold and farming enterprises. As a result of these tragic events and the denial of absolution in confession, Las Casas was prompted to confront his own spiritual blindness, and he began to see the indigenous peoples more fully as the Other.

Las Casas's experiences of the indigenous Other began in his youth. His initial blindness was first occasioned in 1493, when at the age of nine he caught sight of the indigenous Other and watched curiously as Columbus triumphantly paraded seven Tainos through Las Casas's native city of Seville.[4] Then at age fourteen in 1498—and

3. A *repartimiento* is an administrative allotment of indigenous people to Spaniards in an encomienda. Adorno, *Polemics of Possession*, 76, 100. See also Borges, *Quién era Bartolomé*, 27–28.

4. Las Casas, *Historia de las Indias*, bk. 1, ch. 58.

having completed his studies in Latin and letters at Seville's cathedral school—Bartolomé received a Taino teenage boy as a "gift" from his merchant father, Pedro de Las Casas (who had just returned from Hispaniola). This indigenous boy (whom they named Juanico) was to be Las Casas's companion as the young Sevillian began initial canon law studies in Salamanca in preparation for the secular priesthood.[5]

In 1501, Las Casas received the minor orders and the tonsure; in 1502, at age eighteen, he immigrated to the land of the Tainos to work for four years as a *doctrinero* (catechist) and as a provisioner in his father's business.[6] Allegedly, the Sevillano "procured slaves [there], worked with them in the mines, and attended to the cultivation of his [family's] estates."[7] Following his 1507 ordination to the secular priesthood in Rome at age twenty-three, the young priest returned to the Americas, where he served as a chaplain and became an encomendero.

Although Las Casas was reportedly benevolent in his treatment of the encomendado indigenous Other, his conscience was deeply troubled and his lifestyle profoundly challenged by the Dominican friar's refusal to grant him God's pardon in the Sacrament of Penance and Reconciliation. His disturbed conscience straddled the tension between his pursuit of temporal success and his aspiration for eternal salvation; he stood on the threshold of the divide between heaven and hell. His heart weighed heavily as he wrestled with the sufferings of the indigenous peoples and with the suffering in his own heart as he longed for an intimacy with God that was denied him by the Dominican friar's refusal to grant him absolution. These poignant experiences and moral challenges—along with the Hispaniola Dominicans' call for justice during Advent of 1511 in the denunciatory sermon

5. In late June 1500 Queen Isabel ordered that the indigenous peoples, which included Juanico, be returned to the Indies with the new governor and *visitador* Francisco de Bobadilla. Vickery, *Bartolomé de Las Casas*, 32.
6. Giménez Fernández cited Las Casas's own account stating that he received the tonsure in 1501. He contended that Las Casas received the tonsure at that time because of his knowledge of Latin. See "Fray Bartolomé," in Friede and Keen, *Bartolomé de Las Casas*, 70. Manuel Giménez Fernández and Helen Rand Parish (interview by the author, Berkeley, CA, February 12, 2001) both contended that Las Casas received the minor orders of acolyte, porter, lector, and exorcist, which allowed him to act as church sacristan before his first trip to the Indies. Pérez Fernández contended that it was later. *Inventario*, 183–88.
7. MacNutt, *Bartholomew de Las Casas*, 34.

delivered by Friar Antón de Montesinos—contributed greatly to Las Casas's profound conversion in 1514 while meditating on various verses from Sirach (Ecclesiasticus) 34, which read,

> One who slays a son in his father's presence—whoever offers sacrifice from the holdings of the poor. The bread of charity is life itself for the needy; whoever withholds it is a murderer.

> Qui offert sacrificium ex substantia pauperum, quasi qui victimat filium in conspectu patris sui. Panis egentium vita pauperum est: qui defraudat illum homo sanguinis est.[8]

In response, Bartolomé first cut off what shackled him by dispossessing his farms, mines, and indigenous workers in both Hispaniola and Cuba—that is, he made restitution in the form of restorative justice. In his subsequent sermons he specifically linked justice with restitution and eternal salvation and explained to his congregation that "he himself, knowing the danger in which he lived, had released [his] Indians."[9] He informed the Spaniards that they too were obliged in justice to make restitution and that they could not receive absolution in confession if they did not free the indigenous inhabitants they held.

Subsequently, Las Casas became a dedicated collaborator with and a spokesperson for the Hispaniola Dominicans; together they were devoted to the common cause of justice. These mendicants' bold use of the sacrament, prophetic preaching, austere lifestyle, and learned approach to justice issues also prompted Las Casas's conversion and characterized his efforts for the rest of his life.[10] In addition to the

---

8. The full quote from his *Historia de las Indias* is as follows: "El cual, estudiando los sermones que les predicó la pasada Pascua, o otros por aquel tiempo, comenzó a considerar consigo mismo sobre algunas autoridades de la Sagrada Escritura, y, si no me he olvidado, fue aquella la principal y primera del Eclesiástico, capítulo 34, 'Inmolantes ex iniquo oblatio est maculata, et non sunt beneplacitae subsannationes impiorum. Dona iniquorum non probat Altissimus, nec respicit in oblationes iniquorum. Qui offert sacrificium ex substantia pauperum, quasi qui victimat filium in conspectu patris sui; panis egentium vita pauperis est: qui defraudat illi homo sanguinis est. Qui aufert in sudore panem quasi qui occidit proximum suum. Qui effundit sanguinem et qui fraudem facit mercennario, fratres sunt'" (bk. 3, ch. 79). All English biblical quotations hereafter are from the New American Bible (NAB), and all Latin biblical quotations are from the Vulgate.

9. G. Gutiérrez, *Las Casas*, 53; Las Casas, *Historia de las Indias*, bk. 3, ch. 79.

10. See Frades Gaspar, *Uso de la Biblia*, 21.

Dominicans, the young secular priest also received support from the Franciscan friars who had arrived in 1505 from the province of Picard in Belgium. Indeed, in their joint "Carta al rey," these two mendicant groups commended the young secular cleric and informed the emperor that "in these parts, God Our Lord has stirred the spirit of a cleric called Bartolomé de Las Casas. . . a person of truth and virtue, and a special servant and friend of God, most zealous for His law."[11] More specifically, as part of this collaboration and on the recommendation of the Dominican prior Pedro de Córdoba (1460–1521), who was Las Casas's spiritual godfather, the young secular cleric returned to Spain in 1515 with Friar Montesinos. Las Casas's mission was to inform the Crown and church officials about the atrocities taking place in the Indies.

There Las Casas initiated his lifelong battle for justice on behalf of the indigenous people and his search for a "total remedy." As he stated to Pedro de la Rentería (his business partner in Cuba), he sought "nothing less than the total remedy for the Indians doomed to destruction."[12] For this, he appealed first to the ailing monarch. After Ferdinand I's death, Las Casas took his reform plans to the new administration, namely, the aging co-regent, Cardinal Francisco Jiménez de Cisneros, OFM, Ferdinand I's designee; and the figurehead co-regent, Adrian of Utrecht, Charles I's designee.

Writing in accord with the juridical literary genre of *memoriales*, Las Casas (now a *bachiller*) presented the co-regents with the first of three major and officially sanctioned *memoriales* proposing reform plans that he sought to execute as remedies for the injustices.[13] In his seminal work, denominated "Memorial de remedios para las Indias" (1516), he clearly designated salvation as the principal end to which

11. De Córdoba, "Carta al rey," in Pacheco and De Cárdenas, *Colección de documentos inéditos*, 11:221.
12. Alvarez, "Fray Bartolomé," 17; Bataillon, "*Clérigo* Casas," in Friede and Keen, *Bartolomé de Las Casas*, 360, 421n30.
13. That Las Casas also earned the degree of *bachillerato* is attested in two royal documents. In 1516 a royal *cédula*, dated September 16 in Madrid, from the Regents of Castile ordered the officials of the Casa de Contratación in Seville to pay the "Procurador de los Indios, Bachiller Bartolomé de Las Casas" the cost of his journey to the Indies. In 1517 a Certificate of Payment, dated April 6 in Seville, from the treasurer of the House of Trade, Dr. Sancho de Matienzo, stated that Juan Fernández was paid 10,000 maravedís for the passage and the cargo of "Bachiller Bartolomé de Las Casas." Orique, "Unheard Voice of Law," 83.

the Spaniards must lead the indigenous people, and he informed his countrymen that their "primary and ultimate end . . . must be God and to draw them [the indigenous people] to heaven [el primero y último fin . . . ha de ser Dios y a atraerlas al cielo]" by instruction in the Christian faith.[14] For this reason Las Casas opposed the conquests and the enslavement in encomiendas because these unjust pursuits also impeded peaceful evangelization and conversion and thus thwarted possible salvation for the indigenous people.[15] Las Casas also sought to protect new indigenous converts from heresies and heretics by imploring the Crown to send the Santa Inquisición to the Indies.[16]

The young secular cleric further asserted that the indigenous inhabitants were human beings and free—and should be treated as such.[17] This assertion laid the groundwork for his subsequent arguments (beginning in 1519 with the bishop of Darien, Juan de Quevedo) about the full humanity of the indigenous people and their equality as nations and as persons. Additionally, in this 1516 "Memorial de remedios para las Indias," Las Casas unobtrusively but clearly planted the notion that the indigenous people had legal and natural claim to the American land when he asserted,

14. Las Casas, "Remedios para las Indias (1516)," in *Obras escogidas*, 5:27a, 20a, 7a. The first phase of evangelizing in the Antilles relied principally on the collaboration of lay Spaniards in the Crown's vision of Christianization. While Columbus initially sought to simply "convert by love" as he traded gifts with Tainos, in time the navigator noted the possibility of enslaving them. Las Casas, "Diario del primer y tercer viaje de Cristóbal Colón," in *Obras completas*, 14:56. Eventually, the preferred setting for Christianizing became the encomienda. This method was also in accord with the Catholic monarchs' instructions to lead the indigenous peoples "by the example of good works and love." Las Casas, *Las Casas on Columbus*, 7:83. As legislated by the Laws of Burgos, the indigenous people in encomiendas were to be edified by the Spaniards' example of the Christian way of life and instructed in the Christian faith by their encomenderos. This hoped-for peaceful and persuasive method of Christianization would be supported and supplemented by itinerant clergy who served the religious needs of the Spaniards in the missions and churches constructed on the islands.

15. Las Casas also explicitly addressed his concern for the salvation of the Spaniards. See his ""Remedios para las Indias (1516)," in *Obras escogidas*, 5:23a. Later he explicitly addressed his concern for the salvation of the king in his "Carta a un personaje de la corte (1535)," in *Obras escogidas*, 5:63a.

16. Las Casas, "Remedios para las Indias (1516)," in *Obras escogidas*, 5:15a. Seemingly, Las Casas was concerned that unconverted or neophyte indigenous people would be corrupted by certain emigrants who were entering the Americas, such as German Protestants and the alleged false converts from Islam (*moriscos*) and from Judaism (*marranos*).

17. Las Casas, ""Remedios para las Indias (1516)," 5:10a, 24b.

All this should not seem expensive or difficult because, after all, everything comes from them and they work for it and it is theirs . . . and in truth everything belongs to the Indians [anyway].

Todo esto no debe parecer costoso ni grave, porque en fin todo sale dellos y ellos lo trabajan y suyo es . . . y en la verdad todo es de los Indios.[18]

By this, Las Casas also set the tone for his future arguments for restitution and restoration to the indigenous people of what was properly theirs to begin with: their liberty, land, labor, livelihood, and leadership. Indeed, the young secular cleric took his first theoretical and practical step about the duty of restitution when in the 1516 "Memorial de remedios para las Indias" he proposed applying the canon law concept of *amicabilis composito* (amicable settlement) to make restitution by having Spaniards pay in alms for what was owed to all those inhabitants of the Americas who had died.[19]

With his initial reform plan, he made other great strides for change: the 1516 "Memorial de remedios para las Indias" contained fourteen remedial measures; he further detailed peasant and community schemes as alternatives to the encomienda system. Although the implementation of the resultant 1516 Cisneros–Las Casas Reform Plan ended in failure, the proposed towns, or *corregimientos*, of free indigenous people under the Crown eventually became permanent.[20]

In recognition of Las Casas's efforts, the Crown appointed him "Universal Protector of all the Indians in the Indies." At this stage, however, Las Casas did not wholly shed a colonial mentality. Indeed, his reorganized colonization schemes clearly sought to reconcile the interests of Spaniards with the welfare of the indigenous inhabitants—which suggests that he still did not see the indigenous people as the fully autonomous Other.[21]

18. Baptiste, *Thomas More's Utopia*, 61, 45, 57; Las Casas, "Remedios para las Indias (1516)," in *Obras escogidas*, 5:19a, 26a.

19. Las Casas, "Remedios para las Indias (1516)," in *Obras escogidas*, 5:14b; G. Gutiérrez, *Las Casas*, 365.

20. *Corregimientos* consist of populations living in an area subdivided for administrative purposes and under the jurisdiction of a *corregidor* (mayor) appointed by the king.

21. Bataillon, "*Clérigo* Casas," 384–85.

Las Casas's second and third major reform plans were both based on a system of association between free indigenous people and Spanish peasants. His 1518 peasant emigration project, which was approved by the new Spanish king, Charles I, the Flemish-born grandson of the Catholic monarchs, proposed repopulation of the islands with Castilian and Andalusian farmers.[22] His 1518 Tierra Firme reform plan proposed peaceful colonization at Cumaná (Venezuela).[23] To fund the peasant-farmer project, Las Casas requested and was denied financial support from the Council of the Indies.[24] This setback constituted one of the major reasons why this 1518 project was never realized as Las Casas envisioned. However, the plan was not a complete failure, because the Peasant Statutes granting special privileges and exemptions to farmer emigrants who went to the Indies remained permanent as law.[25]

To fund the reform plan for Tierra Firme, which was first proposed in 1518 and finally approved in 1520, Las Casas suggested that the king have recourse to monetary restitution. He reinterpreted the canonical concept of *amicabilis compositio* to apply it also to the destruction done by the Spaniards. This suggestion was also consonant with the earlier opinion about the need for restitution voiced in 1512 by Matías de Paz, O.P., and his mendicant confreres, the Dominican theologians at San Gregorio: Domingo de Soto and Bartolomé de Carranza y Miranda.[26] Accordingly, Las Casas suggested,

> In order to get the needed monies without your highness having to pay them, you might follow this strategy: since in truth the Christians are those who have done such great damage to Your Highness in destroying a great part of that Tierra Firme and totally scandalizing others, in justice your highness can

22. Las Casas, "Remedios para las Indias (1516)," in *Obras escogidas*, 5:31–35.
23. Las Casas, "Memorial de remedios para la Tierra Firme (1518)," in *Obras escogidas*, 5:35–39.
24. Las Casas, "Petición al gran canciller acerca de la capitulación de Tierra Firme (1519)," in *Obras escogidas*, 5:40–43.
25. Giménez Fernández, *Bartolomé de Las Casas: Capellán*, 2:648; Wagner and Parish, *Life and Writings*, 35–45.
26. Hanke, *Spanish Struggle*, 28–29. Paz was also the first European scholar to argue against applying the Aristotelian theory of natural slavery to the indigenous people. See "Dominio de los reyes," in López de Palacios, *Islas del mar Océano*, 217–19, 221–22, 228.

take all from them for its restoration—at least one fifth of all
the gold and pearls that they had acquired, because they had
been unjustly acquired, and without obliging restitution of all
of it, and in this rely on your highness mercy, even though if
you might take all, you would not sin.

Para sacarse los dineros que son menester sin que vuestra alteza
los ponga, se puede tener este manejo, que pues en la verdad los
cristianos son los que a vuestra alteza han hecho tan gran daño
en destruílle mucha parte de aquella Tierra Firme y escandali-
zar toda la otra, justamente puede vuestra alteza tomalles para
la restauración della, al menos, de cinco partes la una de todo
el oro e perlas que han habido, y sin obligarlos a restitución de
todo ello, y en esto les hace vuestra alteza merced, que aunque
se lo tomase todo no pecaría.[27]

During the two years of negotiations, however, Las Casas's attempt
to incorporate restitution in this manner failed; the needed funds for
this ambitious project eventually came from friends in Seville who
advanced him loans.[28]

The envisioned Cumaná plan in Tierra Firme, which constituted
Las Casas's first experiment in a peaceful and persuasive method of
evangelization, endeavored to prevent the need for future restitution.
According to this plan, only twelve Dominican and twelve Franciscan friars, with the tacit authority and eventual presence of bishops,
along with one hundred peasant settlers, would be involved in the
reduction and peaceful conversion of the indigenous people of the
region.[29] Greedy colonists, rapacious slave raiders, and other corrupt
Spaniards would not be allowed. This bold plan would prevent the
"thefts" of the indigenous people's liberty, land, labor, livelihood,
and leadership. The reality proved otherwise. In November 1520, Las
Casas's expedition set sail from Sanlúcar in Spain.[30] In August 1521,

27. Las Casas, "Remedios para las Indias (1516)," in *Obras escogidas*, 5:33ab.
28. MacNutt, *Bartholomew de Las Casas*, 151. During the lengthy period of
negotiations and preparations for the project, Las Casas also earned a licentiate in
canon law at Valladolid, which was substantiated by three royal documents. Orique,
"Unheard Voice of Law," 87.
29. Fernández Rodríguez, *Dominicos en el contexto*, 77.
30. Wagner and Parish, *Life and Writings*, 60–62; MacNutt, *Bartholomew de Las
Casas*, 152.

the Cumaná mission was established, although fatally compromised in its overly optimistic prospects, logistical shortcomings, and unmet stipulations. In January 1522, the experiment of peaceful reduction, colonization, and evangelization ended tragically, as Spaniards conducted raids and conquered and enslaved the unsuspecting native inhabitants. So closed the period from 1515 to 1522, wherein Bartolomé was first and foremost a secular priest-reformer.

At the end of 1522, Padre Las Casas entered the Dominican Order, where he spent seven years in scriptural, theological, philosophical, and canonistic studies. In the future—as friar and then bishop, his major concerns would continue to be salvation and evangelization, justice and restitution. Rooted in his conviction that the salvation of the indigenous people was the sole reason for Spanish presence in the Americas, he continued to champion peaceful evangelization as an alternative to violent evangelization. For example, in his 1531 "Carta" from Hispaniola to the Council of the Indies, Las Casas proposed a plan for the peaceful reduction and evangelization of Yucatán.[31] In 1533, he demonstrated the efficacy of the peaceful approach in Hispaniola when he spent a month in Bahoruco with the Taino *cacique* (indigenous lord), Guarocuá (known by the Christian name Don Enriquillo), during which time Las Casas peacefully persuaded the cacique to become a loyal Christian vassal of the king.[32] In 1535, Las Casas proposed a peaceful conversion plan for the Desaguadero region of Nicaragua; however, prolonged and irreconcilable controversy with governor Rodrigo de Contreras thwarted its realization. In 1537, he started the pioneering and promising project of peaceful reduction and evangelization of the indigenous inhabitants of Tierra de Guerra (Land of War) in Guatemala. Although the indigenous people of that territory had successfully repelled the advances of would-be Spanish conquerors and colonizers, as will be seen, Las Casas and his Dominican confreres were able to initiate the Christianization of these Mayan people and to see the fruits of peaceful and persuasive methods of evangelization.[33]

In his battle for justice, Las Casas would also progressively focus on the doctrine and practice of restitution in his activities and writings.

---

31. Las Casas, "Carta al consejo de las Indias (January 20, 1531)," in *Obras escogidas*, 5:54ab.
32. Clayton, *Bartolomé de Las Casas*, 172, 229–33.
33. Las Casas, "Carta a un personaje," in *Obras escogidas*, 5:66ab.

FIG. 2 In this portrait drawn and engraved by Enguidanos, Bartolomé de Las Casas, Protector of the Indians, is shown with his bishop's pectoral cross, clerical tonsure, and Dominican habit. Frontispiece to Francis MacNutt, *Bartholomew de Las Casas* (Cleveland: Clark, 1909).

For example, while in Puerto la Plata in 1532, where after he finished his Dominican formation, he was appointed prior of the Dominican community. During this time, Las Casas apparently refused to give absolution in confession to a dying Spanish penitent unless he pledged to release the indigenous people he held in encomienda.[34] This practical application of the doctrine of restitution in a deathbed confession resulted in Las Casas's transfer to Santo Domingo, and in the Hispaniola *Audiencia*'s (tribunal of justice) silencing of the Dominican friar's preaching for two years. Although until he became a bishop in 1543, seemingly this is the only known incident in which Las Casas may have used the Sacrament of Penance and Reconciliation as an ecclesiastical tool to enforce the duty of restitution for the evils and harms done to the indigenous people. Nevertheless, the theme of restitution does appear more frequently in his writings.

Despite these setbacks, Las Casas continued to fight for restitution for the indigenous peoples. In his seminal 1531 "Carta," written in Puerto la Plata to the Council of the Indies, Las Casas succinctly presented a framework for just governance and peaceful conversion; he clearly narrated and stridently condemned the injustices done to the indigenous inhabitants and categorically insisted that the offending Spaniards were also "obliged to make restitution for all the goods and riches that others robbed from these people" (sois obligados a restitución de todos los bienes e riquezas que los otros a estas gentes roban). He specifically addressed the conquests, for which the Spaniards were obligated to make restitution because "in general, until this day, there has never been just war waged by those Christians. . . . [Consequently] they are obliged to make restitution" (no ha habido guerra justa ninguna hasta hoy de parte de los cristianos, hablando en universal. . . . Son obligados a restitución).[35]

Las Casas's in-depth understanding of peaceful evangelization, the evils of wars for conversion, and restitution as necessary for justice was also gradually penned by him as a student-friar from

34. Seemingly scholars differ on what transpired: Friede contends that the Spaniard "accepted the confessor's advice and . . . renounced his slaves and goods"; see "Las Casas and Indigenism," in Friede and Keen, *Bartolomé de Las Casas*, 186. Parish simply states that Las Casas withheld deathbed viaticum—giving the impression that the confessee did not renounce his slaves and ill-gotten goods and so died in mortal sin. See Las Casas, *Bartolomé de Las Casas*, 30.

35. Las Casas, "Carta al consejo (1531)," in *Obras escogidas*, 5:51a, 5:54a.

1524 to 1526.[36] The product of his study, prayer, and experience was a comprehensive theoretical missionary tract titled *De unico vocationis modo omnium gentium ad veram religionem (The Only Way to Draw All People to the True Religion)*.[37] In the twenty-four-page epilogue of the Latin version of *The Only Way*, Las Casas argued at length that restitution was required from all because the wars for conversion were mindless, tyrannical, and unjust; accordingly, to engage in such wars was mortal sin. Furthermore, he argued that since all were guilty by commission, cooperation, or counseling, they all must make restoration.[38] His teaching was clear and offered four proofs about the need for restitution:

> One, that all are obliged to make restitution. Two, that this obligation is necessary for salvation. Three, that they are obliged in solidarity; that is, each one for all. Four, that this obligation pertains to all the damages done.

> Primero, que están obligados a restituir. Segundo, que esta obligación es necesaria para la salvación. Tercero, que están obligados solidariamente, esto es, cada uno por todos. Cuarto, que esta obligación abarca todos los daños causados.[39]

In this manner, Las Casas concisely tied restitution (and the restoration of all that was "stolen" from the indigenous people) to justice and salvation in his "Cartas" and, above all, in his missiological treatise, *The Only Way*.

After writing this treatise Las Casas entered a stage of considerable geographic mobility in other regions of the Americas. Indeed,

36. Pérez Fernández, *Inventario*, 201; Barreda, *Ideología y pastoral misionera*, 25–27.

37. In Spanish, this work is titled *Del único modo de atraer a todos los pueblos a la verdadera religión*. The Spanish and Latin (*De unico vocationis modo*) versions are placed on facing pages in *Obras completas* (1524–26), 2:11–557. According to Parish's interpretation of chapter 11, book 3, of Las Casas's *Historia, religionum* meant a "living Faith" in the sense of "doing" the work of religion by deeds that bring about the divine plan of salvation. Parish, interview.

38. Las Casas, *Bartolomé de Las Casas*, 158–82; Las Casas, *De unico vocationis modo*, in *Obras completas*, 2:523–47.

39. Las Casas, *Bartolomé de Las Casas*, 172; Las Casas, "De unico," in *Obras completas*, 2:523.

his tenure at Puerto la Plata and Santo Domingo was followed by six years of travel to, or presence in, regions now regarded as parts of Central America and Mexico. He believed that his arrival in this part of the Indies was providential. Along with Friar Bernardino de Minaya and Friar Pedro de Angulo, Las Casas had volunteered in 1534 for ministry in Peru (which was partially conquered in 1532); together they would accompany the newly appointed bishop of Panama, Tomás de Berlanga.[40] As Las Casas stated of the experience, however, "Our Lord God ordained something other than what we had thought" (Ordenó nuestro Señor Dios otra cosa de la que pensábamos).[41] An ocean calm resulted in their being marooned in mid-1534 in Nicaragua.

Here and throughout these regions, Las Casas continued to witness and condemn the atrocious injustices and to promulgate and apply *The Only Way* of Christianizing—that of convincing the intellect through cogent explanation and persuading the will through good example. In Granada, Nicaragua, he repeatedly saw and vigorously denounced the public floggings and massive exportations of indigenous slaves. His hope to convert peacefully the free indigenous people of the Desaguadero region was also thwarted by the governor's planned armed foray into the region.[42] Las Casas preached against this expedition and threatened to employ another ecclesiastical tool: excommunication of all who might participate.[43] Because Las Casas and his confreres realized that the situation under Governor Contreras was becoming increasingly dangerous and life threatening, they prudently accepted the invitation of bishop-elect Francisco Marroquín to serve in Guatemala.[44] There, beginning in June 1536, they ministered to the spiritual needs of the Spaniards in Santiago de Guatemala and instructed indigenous people in the Christian faith. During this time, Las Casas journeyed to Mexico City to transfer his affiliation from the Hispaniola Dominican province of Santa Cruz to

40. At that time, Peru was included in the diocese of Panama.

41. Las Casas, "Carta a un personaje," in *Obras escogidas*, 5:59b.

42. See Las Casas's 1535 "Carta a un personaje," from Granada, Nicaragua, in *Obras escogidas*, 5:59–68.

43. In ecclesial parlance, excommunication prohibits persons from fulfilling any office or function in, and receiving any other benefits from, the church.

44. Rodrigo de Ladrada, O.P. (who labored in Nueva Granada), and Pedro de Angulo, O.P. (who came from Mexico), joined Las Casas (who came from Hispaniola) in Nicaragua; they later worked together in Guatemala.

MAP 1 Diego Ribero, *Mapa portolano*, 1529. This pilot's map details the coast of the Americas. Library of Congress, Washington, DC, G3200 1529 .R5 MLC.

the Mexican Dominican province of Santiago and to participate in the
1536 Dominican chapter. In January 1537, he returned to Guatemala
as vicar of the Order's missions there and, in time, also became episcopal vicar of Marroquín's diocese.[45]

Las Casas's penchant for writing also continued, as did his focus
on salvation and evangelization, justice, and restitution. For example,
he summarized and distributed a Spanish version of his Latin
De unico vocationis modo (*The Only Way*). This version would have
exposed non-Latin readers, such as governors and conquistadors,
to the necessity for (and the doctrine of) restitution, as well as for
justice and peaceful evangelization. In 1536, he contributed greatly to
the three *actae* (documents) generated at the Mexican ecclesiastical
junta, which he attended as the delegate of bishop-elect Marroquín.[46]
The first *acta* pertained to the Amerindian Church and resulted in
Paul III's 1537 papal decree *Altitudo divino consilii* (The height of
divine counsel). This decree also utilized Las Casas's *Programa para
el modo de vivir de los Indios Cristianos* (Program for the way of life
of Christian Indians) and his memorandum concerning the controversy over the baptism of adult indigenous people. The second acta
dealt with freeing slaves—that is, restoring their freedom by abolishing the injustices suffered and the encomienda. This acta produced
the papal brief *Pastorale officium* (Pastoral office), which reflected
Friar Bartolomé's *Ocho proposiciones contra las conquistas* (Eight
statements against the conquests) and advocated excommunication
of those who enslaved indigenous people and refused to free them.[47]
The third and principal acta concerned evangelization and was based
essentially on Las Casas's *De unico vocationis modo* (*The Only*

45. Giménez Fernández, "Fray Bartolomé," in Friede and Keen, *Bartolomé de Las
Casas*, 89–92.

46. Juntas consisted of civil, religious, or mixed assemblies. During the early colonial period (and specifically—for the purpose of this study—from 1524 to 1546), the
assemblies of bishops, religious, secular clerics, civil functionaries, and prominent colonists were referred to as "ecclesiastical juntas." In 1546, after the establishment of the
three ecclesiastical provinces of Santo Domingo, Mexico, and Lima, these assemblies
were known as synods. Gil, "Las Juntas Eclesiásticas," 7.

47. Promulgated on May 29, 1537, *Pastorale officium*, a companion document for
Sublimis Deus, outlines specific penalties (principally, excommunication) for Christians who enslaved indigenous people. The document was actually meant to enforce a
decree against enslaving indigenous populations issued in 1530 by Charles V. But after
complaints to Charles V, *Pastorale officium* was annulled in 1538.

Way) in its championing of peaceful and persuasive methods of evangelization (and ultimately salvation), as well as in its denouncing of the injustice of the wars and its mandating of the duty of restitution. This *acta principal* also inspired the 1537 landmark papal bull *Sublimis Deus* (From God on high)—the papal encyclical that is often called the Magna Carta of indigenous rights. In this papal encyclical Pope Paul III proclaimed that the indigenous people were fully human, eminently capable of receiving the Christian faith, and completely entitled to their liberty and property, even though they may not be members of the church. Their freedom and lands must be restored, the pope proclaimed.

Back in Guatemala in 1537, the heads of the Spanish colony challenged Las Casas to subdue any indigenous group by putting into practice his theory of peaceful evangelization. Las Casas chose to do so in a hostile, unconquered region, known to the Spaniards as Tierra de Guerra. First, he sent Christianized indigenous itinerant merchants into Sacapula country, where they introduced the people to the doctrines of the Christian faith by incorporating the beliefs in chants and musical couplets. Then, in collaboration with his Dominican confreres and converted caciques, Las Casas extended their evangelization efforts into Quiché. By the year's end Las Casas, Friar Pedro de Angulo, and Friar Rodrigo de Ladrada (Las Casas's faithful companion), along with cacique Don Juan and a retinue of seventy indigenous persons, made contact with the native residents and caciques of Quiché. Together they began a pioneering experiment of peaceful evangelization—one devoid of forced conversion, devastating war, and intrusive colonization.[48]

Las Casas and Ladrada would have continued to live in the territories of Tezulutlán and Cobán had not Bishop Marroquín urgently requested in May 1538 that some friars go to Spain to recruit Dominicans and Franciscans for his diocese. Since arrangements for this would be made at the August 1539 Dominican Provincial Chapter in Mexico City, Las Casas and Ladrada spent from May until

---

48. The friars did succeed in establishing a village of one hundred houses at a place called Rabinal for these normally seminomadic mountain people. Additionally, they enlisted the help of Friar Luis de Cáncer, who was fluent in the Quiché language and who in time converted the chief cacique of Quiché. For a detailed account of the peaceful reduction of Tierra de Guerra, see MacNutt, *Bartholomew de Las Casas*, 190–98, 232.

August 1539 in the southern Mexican region of Oaxaca.[49] There Las Casas began drafting a very long and detailed chronological account that eventually became known as the *Larguísima relación* (Very long account) and copiously documented the evils and harms done in the Indies since the arrival of the Spaniards—all of which demanded restitution.

That same year, in Mexico City, Friar Las Casas attended an ecclesiastical junta called by Viceroy Antonio de Mendoza to discuss indigenous baptisms and other church policies.[50] He also collaborated with Mendoza in several peaceful missions to distant provinces in northwest Mexico. Writing seemingly in response to rising tensions between royal and ecclesiastical powers over the issue of slavery that was generated by Charles V's 1538 prohibition of the publication in the Indies of Pope Paul III's *Sublimis Deus*, Las Casas also prepared a second version of *The Only Way*, titled *How the Kings of Spain Must Care for the World of the Indies viz., [by] the Only Way of Calling All People to a Living Faith* (*De cura habenda regibus Hispaniarum circa orbem Indianum et [sic sc.] de unico vocationis modo omnium gentium ad veram religionem*).[51]

In 1540, with recommendations from civil and ecclesial authorities, Las Casas and Ladrada, as well as their Dominican confrère Luis de Cáncer, returned to Spain with the official mandate of recruiting missionaries for Guatemala and of securing support for peaceful evangelization methods.[52] Once there, Las Casas pursued an addi-

49. Parish and Weidman, *Las Casas en México*, 42.
50. Antonio de Mendoza (1495–July 21, 1552) served as the first viceroy of New Spain from April 17, 1535, to November 25, 1550; then he was appointed the second viceroy of Peru from September 23, 1551, to July 21, 1552. When the Emperor Charles V promulgated the New Laws abolishing slavery and gradually abolishing the encomienda, Mendoza, who was an ally of the encomenderos, was both unable and unwilling to enforce these laws in the face of rigorous opposition from the holders of the encomienda grants.
51. Sometime between 1552 and 1559 at the College of San Gregorio at the University of Valladolid, Las Casas also published another version of his *De unico vocationis modo omnium gentium ad veram religionem*. For the different stages of and audiences for his writing about peaceful evangelization, see Las Casas, *Bartolomé de Las Casas*, 211–21; Pérez Fernández, *Cronología*, 510; Pérez Fernández, *Inventario*, 272; Iglesias Ortega, *Bartolomé de Las Casas*, 325; and Castañeda Delgado, "Doctrinas sobre la coacción," in Las Casas, *Obras completas*, 2:xxvii.
52. In anticipation of the friars' meeting with Charles V, Francisco Marroquín, the bishop of Guatemala, wrote the emperor in 1539 that Las Casas and Ladrada "are servants of God. . . . I have lived with them for more than three years, and daily I have

tional objective that he had desired for almost two decades: to report in person to Emperor Charles V about "most important matters related to the royal estate of the Indies," which urgently required reform measures.[53]

In 1542, Las Casas finally met with Charles V. He first informed the emperor, and then the specially convened junta, of the atrocities and killings taking place in the Americas. Las Casas's oral narrations, written accounts, and legal *probanzas* (evidence) about the injustices included his shocking *Larguísima relación* of the evils and harms done. During Las Casas's presentation, the junta sat spellbound hour by hour, day after day, week after week, during the late spring of 1542, as he read his compelling account of the injustices suffered by the indigenous people and stories of brutality, blindness, and greed. (During this same time Charles V mandated a special investigation of the Council of the Indies after learning from Las Casas about the injustices done by members of the council.) The Dominican friar also presented the junta with another "Memorial de remedios."[54]

Las Casas continued these marathonic days at court with a reading from another of his voluminous writings, the "Entre los remedios" (Among the remedies). In this treatise, he articulated twenty reasons to prove why the indigenous people should not be given to the Spaniards in encomienda. He regarded the eighth remedy as the "one true remedy" from which "all others are derived": the eradication of servitude and slavery in the Americas.[55] In the entirety of this treatise on the encomiendas, he insisted on the indigenous people's right to liberty and therefore to their own lands and governance, which he contended could not be negated by pontifical concessions. He called for their protection as free subjects and vassals of the Crown, whose direct jurisdiction depended on the consent of the governed—that is, of the indigenous people. He demanded the end of encomiendas and

seen their hearts and minds growing in solicitude for the welfare and salvation of these people." He added that "through an experience of more than thirty years, they have come to know and appreciate the hardships these people suffer and what must be done for them." Ladrada remained Las Casas's good friend and faithful companion until Las Casas's death in 1566. Sáenz de Santa María, *Licenciado don Francisco Marroquín*, 162.

53. Las Casas, "Carta al emperador (1540)," in *Obras completas*, 13:99.
54. Las Casas, "Memorial de remedios (1542)," in *Obras escogidas*, 5:120–23.
55. Las Casas, "Entre los remedios," in *Obras escogidas*, 5:91–93. This is why this treatise, which spans pages 69 to 119, is also referred to as *El octavo remedio*.

repartimientos, of conquests and violent evangelization methods, and insisted that the salvation of all, indigenous persons and Spaniards alike, depended on the reestablishment of justice—for which restitution was necessary.

As that intense summer progressed, Las Casas continued to offer guidance to the junta's deliberations by a clarifying *Conclusiones sumarias sobre el remedio de las Indias* (Summary conclusions concerning the remedy of the Indies). His concise and culminating *Parecer* (Opinion) reiterated the major issues requiring legislation: the indigenous people's status as vassals of the Crown, the settlements of the Spaniards, the abolition of slavery, the character of conquests and of future discoveries, and the necessity of peaceful evangelization in word and deed.[56] Toward this same pedagogical end, Las Casas presented the emperor with another document—his "Representación al emperador Carlos V" (On behalf of [others] to the emperor Charles V), in which the Dominican friar argued that canonical justice obliged the conquistadors to make restitution. Las Casas also outlined how payments of restitution should be made to the indigenous people or, if there were no native survivors, to the church for its enterprise of peaceful evangelization. As such, this "Representación" would serve in time as a beginning draft or first manuscript of his future *Confesionario* or *Doce reglas* (Twelve rules).[57] In the autumn of 1542, as a result of Las Casas's persistent appeal to the highest authority and his consistent recourse to the law—whether divine, natural, or human (canonical or civil)—the New Laws, titled *Las leyes y ordenanzas nuevas para la gobernación de las Indias y buen tratamiento y conservación de los Indios* (*Laws and Ordinances Newly Made for the Governance of the Spanish Colonies in the Indies and the Good Treatment and Preservation of the Indians*) were created, elaborated, promulgated, and signed. Twenty-three of the fifty-four articles in the legislation pertained to providing protection and freedom for the

56. This *Parecer* was mistakenly titled "Memorial de remedios (1542)" in *Obras escogidas*, 5:120–23. See Orique, "New Discoveries."

57. Las Casas, "Representación al emperador Carlos V (1543)," in *Obras escogidas*, 5:123–33. During the crafting of the 1542 New Laws, Las Casas was also asked to write a summary of his *Larguísima relación* for the benefit of the young prince Philip; herein lies the genesis of the very brief and famous account narrating and condemning the injustices done by the Spaniards (and Germans) in the Indies: the *Brevísima relación de la destruición de las Indias*.

indigenous people as well as limiting the power of encomenderos. Article 26 prohibited the enslavement of natives, including forced labor in mines and pearl fisheries. Article 27 promulgated their status as vassals of the Crown and not as private individuals. Article 31 proscribed new encomiendas and the holding of encomiendas by public officials and institutions and by secular and religious clergy. Article 35 forbade the inheritance of old encomiendas.[58]

Additionally, in February 1543, before the emperor left Spain, Las Casas and Ladrada presented Charles V with another memorial—one of amendments to clarify aspects of the New Laws and make them more effective.[59] Using scholastic distinctions, they clarified that the type of sovereignty held by the king of Spain was at best *in potentia* and that whether the king's sovereignty became *in actu* would depend on the free consent of the governed—of the indigenous people. This clarification in essence called for the restoration of indigenous sovereignty and for their liberty based on the natives' right to choose or reject the universal lordship of the Spanish monarch. To expedite this full restitution, the two friars suggested that a commission consisting of learned and experienced friars along with loyal royal officials negotiate a contract between the emperor and the indigenous lords that was "in accord with the law, reason, and justice."[60] Other amendments to tighten the enforcement of the New Laws included giving the natives' tributes to their own lords and providing for poor settlers who did not hold encomiendas by employing them in minor royal offices or giving them part of the Crown tribute monies.[61] Subsequently, in June 1543, as regent of the Indies, Prince Philip, the future king, issued a revised version of the New Laws that clarified parts of this legislation and incorporated some of Las Casas and Ladrada's amendments.[62] Given these kinds of watchful interventions and substantive contributions to the initiation and production of this significant legislation that abolished slavery and

58. Simpson, *Encomienda in New Spain*, 129–32.

59. Las Casas, "Memorial de Fray Bartolomé de Las Casas y Fray Rodrigo de Andrada al rey (1543)," in *Obras escogidas*, 5:181–203. The surnames "Andrada" and "Ladrada" were used interchangeably.

60. Rivera-Pagán, *Violent Evangelization*, 70.

61. Clayton, *Bartolomé de Las Casas*, 283.

62. Wagner and Parish, *Life and Writings*, 120.

the encomienda, it can truly be said that Las Casas indeed "made" the 1542 New Laws of the Indies.[63] In other words, the New Laws constituted another and more comprehensive remedy envisioned by Las Casas for the injustices suffered by the indigenous peoples and nations.

Whether as a reward from Las Casas's supporters to honor him or as a punishment from his foes to get him away from court, the Dominican friar was secretly nominated in March 1543 for the wealthy bishopric of Cuzco, Peru. Instead, Las Casas asked for the impoverished diocese of Chiapa—which included southern Mexico, northern Guatemala, and the beloved territory of his peaceful evangelization experiment in Tierra de Guerra.[64] The following year, on March 30, Las Casas was consecrated bishop of Chiapa in the Dominican Church of San Pablo in Seville. His stated goals for the model diocese he intended to build were threefold: colonization by Spanish peasant immigrants with a contingent of friars as overseers, peaceful conversion and reduction of unconquered indigenous people, and protection of conquered natives from Spanish abuses through the enforcement of the 1542 New Laws, which so significantly championed a comprehensive application of the doctrine and practice of restitution.

Having set sail from Sanlúcar, Spain, in early July 1544 and after stopping at the Canary Islands and Santo Domingo, Las Casas and his entourage arrived in his diocese on January 5, 1545, at the port of Lázaro on the coast of San Francisco de Campeche in the province of Yucatán. Hostile Spaniards in this province believed that their bishop instigated the New Laws, whose ordinances they did not intend to keep. Nevertheless, Bishop Las Casas pursued his diocesan goals; for example, in his Epiphany sermon, the new Dominican prelate preached on the injustice and sin of slavery and spoke zealously on the obligation to free the slaves and to provide for their humane

---

63. Pérez Fernández was the first to contend that "it can be said straight out that the one who made the New Laws was Father Las Casas, and nobody else" (Se puede decir a boca llena que quien hizo las Leyes Nuevas fue el Padre Las Casas, y nadie más). *Derecho Hispano-Indiano*, 259.

64. At the time of Las Casas's appointment, the diocese of Chiapa was augmented to include most of Yucatán, Soconusco on the Pacific coast, and the provinces of Tuzulutlán and Lancandón. Clayton, *Bartolomé de Las Casas*, 288. This boundary change diminished the size of Guatemala's diocese and may have been part of the source of Marroquín's precipitous "parting of ways" with Las Casas about this time.

treatment and conversion as mandated by the law of God and the emperor. Escalating tensions culminated as the Spaniards withheld food and supplies from the friars, as well as tithes from their bishop. This and other miserable treatment from the Spanish colonists necessitated the Dominican friars and bishop curtailing their stay in Campeche and departing for the seat of Las Casas's diocese, Ciudad Real de Chiapa, also known as Chiapa de los Españoles.

After a sojourn in Tabasco, Las Casas and his greatly reduced contingent of friars, laypersons, and deacons arrived at Ciudad Real on March 21, 1545.[65] At first, the reception was cordial: they received assistance to establish a temporary convent and access to donations of food and supplies. Even so, the indigenous people brought continual tales of suffering and daily appeals for protection to Las Casas. The bishop also observed the brutal treatment of the indigenous people and the excessive tributes levied on them, as well as the colonists' noncompliance with the New Laws. Indeed, in Ciudad Real, where the majority of the population of his diocese lived, slavery flourished. Bishop Las Casas tried systematically to secure the colonists' compliance with the New Laws and with the divine law to love one's neighbor by private conversations with principal offenders, by argument, by explanation of the New Laws, and by public preaching and exhortations—all to no avail.

On Passion Sunday in 1545, Bishop Las Casas prepared his flock for Holy Week—for the solemn week preceding the celebration of Christ's passion. After he reminded his flock of their annual duty to confess their sins, he announced that absolution in confession would not be given to those who retained slaves.[66] He then named confessors for slaveholding penitents: the cathedral dean, Gil de Quintana; the cathedral canon, Juan de Perera; and Dominican friars Tomás Casillas, Tomás de la Torre, Alonso de Villabra, and Domingo de Arana.[67] He furnished these designated confessors with a detailed list

65. Originally, Las Casas's entourage consisted of forty-five friars, lay brothers, and deacons, but their numbers were drastically reduced by disease (some during the voyage), death (nine drowning in the shipwreck), and desertion (nineteen at the ports of call en route).

66. According to the Julian Calendar, Passion Sunday was on March 29, and the Holy Week Triduum fell on the following days: Thursday (April 2), Friday (April 3), and Saturday (April 4); Easter Sunday of that same year was April 5. The Gregorian Calendar was introduced in 1582.

67. Las Casas, "Proclamación a los feligreses de Chiapa (March 20, 1545)," in Obras escogidas, 5:215–18.

of cases with which they would be confronted. (This list probably corresponded to the categories specified in Las Casas's future *Doce reglas*.) As a result, all hell broke loose. The Spaniards' uproar was echoed by the local Mercedarian clerics and by Quintana (who was excommunicated by Las Casas and then fled to Guatemala). The angry colonists appealed to civil authorities and threatened to appeal to Mexico's archbishop as well as to the pope. Someone even fired a musket shot into the bishop's room! And, for the second time, the Dominican friars were denied food and supplies!

Long story short, the friars moved to Chiapa de los Indios, where they established a convent. Meanwhile, Bishop Las Casas began his journey to Gracias a Dios in Honduras to attend the consecration of the bishop-elect of Nicaragua, Antonio Valdivieso, O.P. En route, Las Casas spent time at Tierra de Guerra, seemingly in May and June of 1545, where the indigenous people's flourishing Christian life comforted and cheered him. Subsequently, in Gracias a Dios, which in 1544 had become the provisional seat of the Audiencia de los Confines, he presented a seven-article memorial to the Audiencia that listed the different ways that this civil authority could enforce the New Laws. They laughed at him, called him a lunatic, and denied his request—most likely because, between the Audiencia president Maldonado and his associates, they owned a total of sixty thousand slaves. During this time, as in Ciudad Real (Chiapa de los Españoles), the bishop of Chiapa remained serene and resolute in the face of insults, indignities, opposition, and threats. Subsequently, Bishop Las Casas and Bishop-Elect Valdevieso reported the Audiencia's conduct and noncompliance to Prince Philip, with the result that the Audiencia did eventually agree to send auditor Juan Rogel to Ciudad Real to assure that the New Laws were executed.[68]

In December 1545, Las Casas began his return to Ciudad Real— not knowing that, in response to petitions and arguments received by the Crown, the most important parts of the New Laws had been abrogated by the emperor on November 24. Meanwhile, Las Casas's Dominican confreres as well as the Spanish colonists in Ciudad Real separately monitored the whereabouts of the bishop. The Dominicans

---

68. Las Casas, "Carta de Fray Bartolomé de Las Casas, obispo de Chiapa y de Fray Antonio de Valdivieso, obispo de Nicaragua, al Príncipe Don Felipe (October 25, 1545)," in *Obras escogidas*, 5:223.

begged him not to put his life in danger by returning to the seat of his diocese. Bishop Las Casas's response was

> Here I wish to remain, this church is my spouse, she is not mine to abandon. This is the fortress of my residence. I wish to irrigate it with my blood; if they might take my life, so that the earth is soaked in the zeal of service for God that I have, and that it may remain fertile to bear the fruit that I desire—that is, the end of the injustice that stains and possesses [the earth].

> Aquí me quiero estar, esta iglesia es mi esposa,
> no la tengo de desamparar; este es el alcázar de mi residencia,
> quiérole regar con mi sangre, si me quitaren la vida,
> para que se embeba en la tierra el celo del servicio
> de Dios que tengo y quede fértil para dar el fruto que yo deseo,
> que es el fin de la injusticia que la mancha y posee.[69]

The colonists readied for this—his second arrival in Ciudad Real— by compiling a formal notification that their prelate must abandon his stand and follow the example of other bishops in the colonies until the emperor's decision about their concerns was known . . . or they would suppress his tithes. In response to the notification, Bishop Las Casas assured the Spaniards that he had no intention of interfering with their properties except insofar as was necessary to prevent sin against God and their neighbor.[70] To that end, he again confirmed the cathedral canon and the four Dominicans as confessors for slaveholders. Additionally, as demanded by the Ciudad Real City Council, he also gave faculties to hear slaveholders' confessions to a Mercedarian friar and a Guatemalan cleric, even though the Dominican friars questioned their integrity. Bishop Las Casas also gave his vicar-general instructions to impose interdiction—another ecclesiastical tool—on anyone who disobeyed his orders.[71]

Given the tumult of continuous hostilities from the Spanish colonists, as well as the summons from *visitador* (superintendent)

69. Fabié, *Vidas y escritas*, 1:182.
70. Fabié, *Vida y escritos*, 1:18, 258–60, 264.
71. Generally speaking, in ecclesial understanding, interdiction prohibits reception of the sacraments (except confession and viaticum) and participation in the liturgy and the Divine Office.

Francisco Tello de Sandoval to attend an ecclesiastical synod in
Mexico City and the arrival of auditor Rogel to enforce the New
Laws, Las Casas surely sensed that his departure from his diocese
was imminent and perhaps permanent.[72] Accordingly, he planned to
depart Ciudad Real with friars Rodrigo de Ladrada, Vicente Ferrer,
and Luis de Cáncer as well as Canon Perera during the first week
of Lent in March 1546, and then all would stay in Antequera in the
province of Oaxaca to wait for the opening of the synod scheduled
for later in the year. This ecclesiastical assembly and the assembly of
members of the religious Orders, which Las Casas arranged, as well
as subsequent developments on both sides of the Atlantic, would
prove significant for the enforcement of the doctrine and practice of
restitution.

72. Note that at this time Las Casas transferred his property to the Dominicans.
Furthermore, Las Casas had seemingly thrice requested a transfer to Verapaz, and
he had suggested that new bishops be assigned for Soconusco, Chiapa, and Yucatán.
In their joint 1545 letter to the prince, Las Casas and Valdivieso also indicated their
determination "to leave [their] bishoprics . . . to seek justice and aid from [His] Maj-
esty . . . and not to return until [the prince] uproots the tyranny." "Carta de Fray Bartolomé," in *Obras escogidas*, 5:223. Francisco Tello de Sandoval, a Spanish ecclesiastic
and administrator, inquisitor in Toledo, and a member of the Council of the Indies, was
sent as a *visitador* to New Spain in 1543. His intent was to promote compliance with
the 1542 New Laws, but some of these laws had already been suspended because of the
opposition of the encomenderos. Upon his return to Spain, he became a chancellor in
Granada (1557) and Valladolid (1559), president of the Council of the Indies (1564),
and bishop of Osma (1567).

2

"I Absolve . . .": A First Brush with the Eternal Flames of Hell

At ten o'clock one morning in June 1546, as Las Casas arrived late for the ecclesiastical synod convoked by Francisco Tello de Sandoval in Mexico City, a penitential silence fell over the assembly, punctuated by confessional-like whispers among the participants. The loud and vocal bishop of Chiapa, who was indeed the instigator and championer of the 1542 New Laws, had joined the synod to argue for solutions to the pervasive and long-standing issues of unjust wars and enslavements, peaceful evangelization and the subsequent conversion of the indigenous peoples, and restitution from the Spaniards to attain their salvation. As will be seen, Las Casas would utilize this synod of bishops in addition to the subsequent junta of mendicant friars to produce the manuscript that eventually became the *Doce reglas para confesores*.[1] Accordingly, this chapter presents the trajectory of the development of this confessionary manuscript from the first written *Doce reglas* in 1546 to its publication in 1552 as an augmented treatise: *Aquí se contienen unos avisos y reglas para los*

1. Since clear and unequivocal information about the juntas in 1546 is unavailable, this study relies on Parish and Weidman's widely lauded *Las Casas en México*. This 1992 publication built on solid research and clarified what took place at the two juntas. With the exception of Remesal's dubious pro-Lascasian history, records about the third ecclesiastical junta have been lost. Fortunately, Parish, in collaboration with Weidman, discovered several new documents and painstakingly researched and carefully reconstructed as best as possible the circumstances surrounding and the outcome of this gathering. As such, this section is indebted to their scholarship. See Parish and Weidman, *Las Casas en México*. This current study also furthers Parish's work by considering the specific use of confession in general and of the *Confesionario* in particular.

confesores, as well as examines the fallout of Las Casas's use of the sacrament as he battled for justice for the indigenous peoples.

This trajectory begins with Las Casas's tardy and unannounced arrival at the ecclesiastical synod that morning. Indeed, Visitador Lic. Tello de Sandoval and Viceroy Antonio de Mendoza had attempted to delay (and perhaps even prevent) Las Casas's arrival. Both of these civil authorities feared possible disturbances between advocates of encomenderos and supporters of Las Casas. The former were angry about the bishop's role in generating the New Laws; the latter were happy with the prelate's care of the indigenous inhabitants, so much so that upon seeing him some unashamedly announced, "Este es el Obispo santo, el verdadero padre de los Indios" (This is the holy bishop, the true Father of the Indians). Consequently, both Sandoval and Mendoza instructed Las Casas to remain at the Dominican priory in Antequera in the valley of Oaxaca until he received their permission to proceed into Mexico City, which he did.[2] Once Las Casas had joined the assembly and was lodged in the Dominican community in Mexico City, the viceroy and the *oidores* (provincial judges) of the Audiencia of New Spain "graciously" sought to welcome the friar-bishop. Their would-be conciliatory, although duplicitous, gesture repulsed Las Casas because, as he informed them, "I have excommunicated the viceroy and members of the Audiencia for having given sentence to cut off the hand of a clergyman [who was convicted of a serious crime] in Antequera."[3] By drawing on priestly privileges of the ancient Romans, the bishop of Chiapa punished their violations of clerical immunity by again employing a tool of ecclesiastical power and authority—that of excommunication.

Participants at this third ecclesiastical assembly of New Spain, who gathered daily during June and July in 1546, included the Dominican bishop of Chiapa; the archbishop of Mexico; the bishops of Guatemala, Oaxaca, Michoacán, and seemingly of Tlaxcala; other prelates and chief theologians of various religious Orders; local secular clerics; and *letrados* (lawyers or the learned) from among colonists,

2. Fabié, *Vida y escritos*, 1:205; Vera, *Compendio histórico*, 2:123.
3. Parish chronicled the triple violation that took place: the violation of sanctuary in a church in which the cleric took refuge, a trial in secular rather than in ecclesial court, and mutilation of a clergyman. Parish and Weidman, *Las Casas en México*, 51–52; Lupher, *Romans*, 124–25.

as well as Sandoval and Mendoza.[4] Ostensibly, the synod's purpose
was to make decisions about the administration of the sacrament of
the Eucharist to neophyte indigenous converts.[5] Las Casas's goal was
to persistently pursue the conversion and welfare of the indigenous
people. Given that portions of the New Laws that prohibited inheritance of encomiendas had been revoked, Las Casas felt that he could
finally pursue this ultimate goal.[6] He was alone in this stand, however, since even his supportive friends, including some bishops and
friars, favored the revocation. Nevertheless, issues about indigenous
rights, tyranny of wars, Spanish imperial sovereignty, peaceful evangelization, and criteria for administering the sacraments to colonists
took center stage. Arguments concerning these issues were defended
or defeated by recourse to the church fathers, to theologians, and to
canonists, as "men of God clashed with haughty feudal-minded over-
lords" in seemingly endless debates.[7]

Initially, Las Casas tried unsuccessfully to convince the assembly
that bishops were obliged to act to relieve the "yoke of the encomienda" that burdened so many indigenous people and to do so using
the sacrament of confession, as he had done during the previous
year in his diocese. In the judgment of the synod's participants, this
strategy was deemed too political. He was told that the Audiencia was
responsible for this matter and that, as a result of the 1545 epidemic,
there was also an acute labor shortage. The assembly also opined that
denying absolution in confession was too rigorous, and encomenderos feared that bishops would be biased because prelates were the
designated Protectors of the Indians.

The synod's many weeks of deliberations eventually resulted in
eight actae. To placate those assembled as well as to keep the churchmen's discussions in the spiritual plane, Las Casas voted in favor of
the first acta (which Parish dubbed an "innocuous statement") about
the king's obligation to provide for the instruction of the indigenous
inhabitants in the Catholic faith. The second acta, which called for
restitution, elicited much discussion from all, but not complete

4. Fabié, *Vida y escritos*, 1:205; Vera, *Compendio histórico*, 2:122; MacNutt, *Bartholomew de Las Casas*, 273; Parish and Weidman, *Las Casas en México*, 57.
5. Vera, *Compendio histórico*, 2:123.
6. This law against the inheritance would have placed the indigenous as free vassals of the king. Parish and Weidman, *Las Casas en México*, 53, 56.
7. Picón-Salas, *Cultural History*, 48.

agreement from the bishop of Chiapa: he objected to the clause that some Spaniards acted *en buena conciencia* (in good conscience). Nevertheless, with this second acta, Las Casas did obtain strong support for the principle and duty of restitution: for what encomenderos owed the indigenous people, for their excessive tributes, and for the Spaniards' neglect of or impediments they placed to the natives' evangelization and conversion. This acta also generated protests from encomenderos and conquerors as well as from functionaries of colonial administration over the curtailment or loss of their rights. More important, this acta was significant because Las Casas's future *Doce reglas* would focus solely and comprehensively on the duty of restitution.[8]

The bishops' synod promulgated two more actae that also directly protected the indigenous people: the third and fourth prohibited forcing them to pay tithes and requiring them to pay for learning about the Christian faith. The final four actae of the synod further bolstered ecclesiastical jurisdiction: the fifth reformed the duties of cathedral chapters (including designating who replaced the bishop or archbishop when absent from his see, as Bishop Las Casas would be); the sixth established the Inquisition in New Spain; the seventh addressed changes in the boundaries of the dioceses of Chiapa and Michoacán, and the eighth reaffirmed ecclesiastical immunity for priests and bishops—a policy that was violated by the treatment of the Antequeran clergyman by the civil authorities. The bishops' unanimous approval of this reassertion of immunity was probably achieved because of Las Casas's preliminary *Parecer* on the subject at the synod. The bishop of Chiapa would certainly need such protection once his future *Doce reglas* manuscript was in the public domain.[9]

Significantly, each of these actae, although belonging to matters of the spiritual sphere, carried implications for the temporal sphere. So too, in the diocese of Chiapa, on March 20, 1545, as Las Casas celebrated Passion Sunday, he spoke against the encomenderos. That is, he threatened their economic status quo, as would his soon-to-be-fully redacted *Doce reglas*; he pointed a finger at all Spaniards engaged in profitable conquest, control, and commerce of indigenous peoples. Furthermore, in the eighth rule of his forthcoming *Doce*

8. Parish and Weidman, *Las Casas en México*, 58–64.
9. Parish and Weidman, 65–69.

reglas manuscript, the bishop of Chiapa explicitly drew on the orders of the 1546 bishops' synod in his advice about restitution for tributes paid.[10] In this manner, the pronouncements of the bishops' synod brokered a broad arena of ecclesiastical power and authority that penetrated deep into the workings of colonists' temporal life, which Las Casas could build on in his recourse to the sacrament of confession to demand restitution for the evils and harms done by all Spaniards in the Indies. He could utilize this sacramental remedy that drew on both the power of the keys and the power of the seal of confession.

From the third ecclesiastical assembly, however, the bishop of Chiapa needed—and requested—deliberation about the prohibition of slavery and the cessation of abusive personal services. Although the viceroy denied the bishop's request, Mendoza did permit him to convene a friars' junta at the Dominican priory, in which religious of the three mendicant Orders could have "as many sessions on as many topics as Las Casas desired." They were asked to determine "what was in keeping with reason and justice." The viceroy also qualified his permission by stipulating (at the urging of the turncoat bishop of Guatemala) that these issues were to be discussed only by the friars and that Las Casas was not allowed to vote. Nevertheless, the indefatigable bishop of Chiapa actively participated in the friars' junta, which reportedly lasted until the first of November. He gave counsel and made available actae from previous ecclesiastical juntas, such as those from 1536, at which *oidores* and churchmen unanimously condemned slavery.[11]

The friars' junta yielded several important Lascasian-like directives. The mendicants unanimously condemned the wars of conquest. They vehemently denounced the enslavement of the indigenous people and the oppressive personal services. They asserted that, with the possible exception of Jalisco, indigenous people had always been

10. Las Casas, *Avisos y reglas*, in *Obras escogidas*, 5:240ab.
11. This change of heart for Mendoza took place as the viceroy listened to a sermon that Las Casas preached on Isaiah chapter 30:8–11, which read, "Now come, write it on a tablet they can keep, inscribe it on a scroll, that in time to come it may be an eternal witness. For this is a rebellious people, deceitful children, children who refuse to listen to the instruction of the Lord, who say to the seers: 'Do not see'; to the prophets, 'Do not prophesy truth for us; speak smooth things to us, see visions that deceive! Turn aside from the way! Get out of the path! Let us hear no more of the Holy One of Israel!'" Parish and Weidman, *Las Casas en México*, 61–62; Carrillo Cázares, *Debate*, 477; Pérez Fernández, *Inventario*, 468.

unjustly enslaved and were to be set free.[12] They firmly resolved not to absolve any Spaniards who were slave owners or abusive encomenderos. Furthermore, in accord with the New Laws, the mendicants required that any title to indigenous slaves must be one examined by the Audiencia—an order that clearly legitimated Las Casas's refusal to absolve the notorious Chiapan slave owners. With the directive from the friars' junta about absolution, coupled with the duty of restitution espoused by the bishops' synod, Bishop Las Casas was now ready to employ the sacrament of confession to generate healing for the indigenous people and to assure the eternal salvation of the Spaniards in the Indies, and, simultaneously, to enforce conformity with the original 1542 New Laws, at least in his diocese of Chiapa, as was his duty as bishop.

At that same time, as stated in the *Argumento* of Las Casas's published *Avisos y reglas,* "several Dominican friars . . . begged and charged . . . [him] . . . several times" to give them some rules to guide them as confessors "in the forum of conscience."[13] Accordingly, in 1546, he finalized the twelve detailed rules instructing how to obligate and assess restitution and whether to grant absolution.[14] These twelve rules, or *doce reglas,* which applied to all conquerors,

12. In early colonial Mexico the most formidable indigenous uprising against Spanish expansion was the Mixtón War, waged from 1540 to 1542. The Spanish and their central Mesoamerican allies (Aztecs and Tlaxcalans) fought against northern indigenous groups (mainly Cazcán, Zacatec, Guachichil, and Huichol); these northern groups resisted entrance into their region to take slaves and pursue silver mining and establish encomiendas. In this war, Spaniards used just-war arguments to justify the capture and enslavement of the indigenous population. Furthermore, the Crown had received a fifth of the large number of the slaves taken in the war, which would have been unacceptable, according to Las Casas's strict rules. Sauer, *Land and Life,* 113–15; Cook, "Muslims and *Chichimeca.*"

13. Las Casas, *Avisos y reglas,* in *Obras escogidas,* 5:235a. Conscience is a judicial power given by God to be the sovereign guide of human actions. Because the sacrament of confession pertained to the spiritual welfare of the individual Christian and one's relationship to God, this forum of penance was also called the forum of conscience. Hill, *Age of Reason,* 26. Confession constitutes a forum of conscience in which truth is sought by examining the conscience of the penitent and by informing the conscience of the priest. Las Casas gave instructions about yearly confession previously in his "Proclamación a los feligreses de Chiapa (March 20, 1545)," in *Obras escogidas,* 5:215–18.

14. Although Remesal asserted that Las Casas's twelve rules were formulated and unanimously approved at the bishops' junta, this is not possible, since Bishop Marroquín opposed the *Confesionario* after it became public. See *Historia general,* bk. 2, pp. 110–11, 165. Neither could Las Casas's manual for confessors have been finalized

encomenderos, slave owners, and merchants, as well as to any others who acquired ill-gotten gain by exploiting indigenous people,
were rooted by Las Casas in three premises: (1) that all the wars of
conquest were unjust; (2) that all enslavement of indigenous people
was unjust, and (3) that all the Spaniards acted in bad faith. Realizing
how subversive his confessors' guide was in its scope and premises,
as well as in its method of execution, which demanded the penitents'
legal oath to make restitution, the bishop of Chiapa strove to keep
the manuscript a strict secret.[15]

For some time, however, Las Casas had realized that he needed
to return to Spain to lobby permanently at court for indigenous
rights—to defend in Spain what he could not defend adequately in
the Indies.[16] Moreover, he had completed the required two years
of residence (of the six-year episcopal term) in his diocese. He had
already appointed Canon Juan de Perera as his vicar-general on
November 9, 1546, and he had ordered interdiction of those who did
not obey Perera.[17] He had already designated Dominican friars as
confessors for the offending Spaniards in Ciudad Real de los Españoles, and he had armed them with copies of the *Doce reglas*.[18]

Additionally, the promulgation of the New Laws had not guaranteed that their legislated ordinances about the conquests and the
grants of encomiendas would be carried out. But if all bishops utilized
the *Doce reglas* to address and resolve the issue of the enslavement
of indigenous peoples, their ecclesiastical power in the spiritual
realm could effect the desired changes in the temporal realm. Consequently, sometime between November 1546 and March 1547, Las
Casas penned an open letter to regent Prince Philip II, titled *Quaestio
theologalis*.[19] In this letter the Dominican bishop generated a forceful defense of the superiority of spiritual power over civil power. His
letter reinforced the affirmation of clerical immunity articulated in
the eighth acta of the bishops' synod—an immunity derived from the

and approved at the friars' junta, since some of the Dominican mendicants needed
clarification of rules 1 and 5. Wagner and Parish, *Life and Writings*, 166.
   15. Parish and Weidman, *Las Casas en México*, 62–65.
   16. Fernández Rodríguez, *Dominicos en el contexto*, 214.
   17. Clayton, *Bartolomé de Las Casas*, 335.
   18. Parish and Weidman, *Las Casas en México*, 61–63; MacNutt, *Bartholomew de
Las Casas*, 276.
   19. Las Casas, *Quaestio theologalis*, in *Obras completas*, 12:262–408.

tradition of combining the religious and civil in one universal order. This immunity would protect the bishops and their priests (when hopefully) they followed the confessionary procedures outlined in the *Doce reglas*. Las Casas's letter, today referred to as "De exemptione sive damnatione" (On exemption or damnation), explicated in clear and simple Latin how "hombres consagrados a Dios" (men consecrated to God) could not by natural and divine law (nor by the law of *ius gentium* governing all peoples of the world) be subject to princes and secular judges. For example, Las Casas cited the case of Bishop Ambrose, who humbled Emperor Theodosius by refusing the ruler's entrance into the Milan cathedral.[20] Las Casas also cited tradition in support of the principle of immunity by reference to priestly privileges among the Israelites and the Romans.[21]

The bishop of Chiapa concluded his cogent and systematic argument by adamantly warning that any secular authority who did not respect this exemption will surely suffer corporal, spiritual, and eternal death. As well, he cautioned the prince to "take care, then, [lest he too] be thrown out of the temple, slayed with the sword of anathema, and wounded by the detestable leper of mortal sin" (Tenga, pues, cuidado . . . ser arrojado del templo, matado por la espada del anatema, y herido por la detestable lepra del pecado mortal).[22]

Having completed the needed arrangements and confident of securing ecclesiastical immunity, Bishop Las Casas left Mexico City. He returned to Oaxaca in early December, then proceeded to Vera Cruz, where he stayed until sailing for Spain in March 1547. He arrived in Lisbon in June, spent the summer in Valladolid, and passed the rest of the year in Aranda de Duero, Monzón. He then journeyed to Alcalá de Henares, where he received a friendly reception at court.[23] There he informed the prince about the happenings in the Indies, including the gross negligence of the Audiencia de los Confines with respect to the New Laws. Documentary evidence

20. Dutton, Findlay, and Wilson, *Theatre and Religion*, 81; Parish and Weidman, *Las Casas en México*, 67.

21. Lupher, *Romans*, 124–26.

22. Parish and Weidman, *Las Casas en México*, 65–69; G. Gutiérrez, *Las Casas*, 319.

23. Friede, "Las Casas and Indigenism," in Friede and Keen, *Bartolomé de Las Casas*, 189, 191. Dates and places of Las Casas's journeys are taken from Pérez Fernández's voluminous studies and, as this preeminent Lascasian scholar cautions, are approximate. See his *Cronología*, 143–45; and his *Inventario*, 495–96.

elucidating Las Casas's activities in Spain shows that he was just as busy between 1547 and 1552 as he was between 1520 and 1546.[24] In addition to sharing his expertise in canon law, theology, and philosophy, as well as his vast eyewitness experience, the bishop of Chiapa remained proactive in his labors and writings on behalf of the indigenous peoples. Surely his attention would have also focused on the various responses to his *Doce reglas*.

One of his first endeavors was to respond to a concern of some Dominican friars who had requested and read the *Doce reglas*. As he noted in the first section of the published *Avisos y reglas*, the concern "of some religious" was with respect to rules 1 and 5, which obliged confessors "to demand that penitents give a suitable and juridical pledge to make restitution" before giving them absolution. Las Casas subsequently acknowledged that "some religious [held] this to be harsh, and [opined that] . . . there is no legal reason for such a pledge."[25] Consequently, he wrote an *Adición* (appendix) to the *Doce reglas*, in which he addressed the first and the fifth rules and demonstrated how the confessor's obligation to require such a juridical document is based on divine, natural, and positive law—both canon and civil.[26]

Other responses to the *Doce reglas* consisted of accusations (probably instigated by Toribio Motolinía) that some phrases and sentences were "false and scandalous." After all, in Las Casas's manuscript of twelve rules, he did call the conquerors *raptores* (kidnappers) in rule 5, as well as tyrants and *predones* (thieves) in rule 11. According to his accusers, he also erroneously portrayed the encomenderos in rules 7–10, as well as the merchants in rule 11.[27] Protests and reactions to *Doce reglas* continued to ensue at local and regional levels from both civil and some ecclesiastical sources. For example, the immediate response from the Mexican *cabildo* (town council) on November 15, 1546, was to send a copy of the original *Doce reglas* (that would have been without the *Adición*) to the Council of the Indies. Refutations generated by Viceroy Mendoza and by

24. Friede, "Las Casas and Indigenism," in Friede and Keen, *Bartolomé de Las Casas*, 192–93; Hanke and Giménez Fernández, *Bartolomé de Las Casas, 1474–1566*, doc. nos. 258–363.

25. Las Casas, *Avisos y reglas*, in *Obras escogidas*, 5:235a.

26. Roa-de-la-Carrera, *Histories of Infamy*, 59.

27. Pérez Fernández, *Fray Toribio Motolinía*, 144–45.

Guatemala's governor, Alonso de Maldonado, as well as by Guatemala's bishop, Francisco Marroquín, were also sent to authorities in
Spain. In 1548, Mendoza publicly burned the manuscript.[28]

Since, as Pérez Fernández pointed out, it could take even a year for
"mail" to arrive at its destination in Spain, the council's reply was
likely a *cédula* (legal document) dated November 28, 1548. At that
time their censors pointed to some "legal technicalities" and discrep-
ancies between the text and the law in rules 1 and 5.[29] These were the
same rules that concerned some of the friars, and to which Las Casas
had responded in his yet-not-public *Adición*. The bishop of Chiapa
seemingly ignored this tardy feedback from the Council of the Indies,
partially because earlier that year during February he had already
submitted his complete manuscript (the *Doce reglas* and the *Adición*)
to six Salamancan theologians and had received their approval of this
revised and augmented version of the *Confesionario*.[30]

Moreover, although the Council of the Indies did not challenge
Las Casas's criticisms of the conquests and encomiendas, they did
order the Audiencias of New Spain and of Los Confines to confiscate
all copies of the manuscript. Scholars also contend that "the seizure,
not the prohibition, of [copies of] the *Doce reglas* was ordered [by the
Council of the Indies] at the urging of Juan Ginés de Sepúlveda"—
who was the mouthpiece for Las Casas's opponents and the most
formidable of all his adversaries.[31] Sepúlveda's role in this seizure is

28. García Icazbalceta, *Colección de documentos*, 1:256. Franciscan friar Motolinía
also said that Mendoza burned the manuscripts. Pérez Fernández pointed out that this
was a personal decision on the part of the viceroy since the order was to send them to
the Council of the Indies; see *Fray Toribio Motolinía*, 115, 143. Scholars opine that the
only manuscript that was prohibited and publicly burned during the life of its author
was Las Casas's *Confesionario* in 1548; see Parish and Weidman, *Las Casas en México*,
63–70; and Adorno, *Polemics of Possession*, 76, 338.

29. Roa-de-la-Carrera, *Histories of Infamy*, 59. In that era, censorship focused on
statements contradicting doctrinal or legal principles.

30. The Dominican theologians were Friar Pedro de Sotomayor and Friar
Francisco de San Pablo, both from the College of San Gregorio; Melchor Cano and
Domingo Galindo from Salamanca; Mancio de Corpus Christi from Alcalá; and Friar
Bartolomé de Carranza y Miranda, who recently returned from the Council of Trent
and who would become the cardinal archbishop of Toledo. Iglesias Ortega, *Bartolomé
de Las Casas*, 58–59.

31. Friede, "Las Casas and Indigenism," in Friede and Keen, *Bartolomé de Las
Casas*, 191, 225n244. Friede refers to prominent Lascasian scholars such as Hanke,
Giménez Fernández, and Losada. See also Fabié's account about Las Casas's adversaries
questioning rule 7, in his *Vida y escritos*, 1:312–15.

plausible, given that, in addition to the controversy over the *Doce reglas* manuscript, Las Casas was also embroiled in the controversy over Sepúlveda's *Democrates secundus*, which justified waging wars of conquest to "christianize" the "naturally inferior" peoples of the Americas.[32]

Another prominent Lascasian scholar contends that, in the autumn of 1548, the Councils of Castile and of the Inquisition requested an explanation from the bishop of Chiapa about an issue in rule 7 of the *Doce reglas*: that of Spanish sovereignty.[33] The tacit challenge to royal authority in rule 7 read, in part,

> all the things that have been done throughout the Indies . . . have been contrary to all natural law and the law of nations, and also against divine law; and therefore is entirely unjust, iniquitous, tyrannical, and deserving of all eternal fire and, consequently, null, invalid, and without any value and weight of law.

> todas las cosas que se han hecho en todas las Indias . . . ha sido contra todo derecho natural y derecho de las gentes, y también contra derecho divino; y por tanto, es todo injusto, inicuo, tiránico y digno todo fuego infernal, y, por consiguiente, nulo, inválido y sin algún valor y momento de Derecho.[34]

This seventh rule, which asserted that all that has been done in the Indies by the Spaniards is without any legal standing, also prompted Sepúlveda to approach the Council of Castile and the Inquisition in

32. Looming in the background at this time, in 1546 or 1547, "Cardinal García de Loaysa (president of the Council of the Indies, a Dominican, no friend of Las Casas and indianists, and the one who allowed the resumption of enslavement) asked Sepúlveda for a learned opinion that wars against the Indians were just." Accordingly, Sepúlveda (1489/90–1573) a Spanish humanist, philosopher, and theologian, wrote *Democrates alter, sive de justis belli causus apud Indos*, which is referred to as *Democrates secundus* (second *Democrates*) because his arguments closely paralleled his 1535 *Democrates primus*. Las Casas lobbied against the publication of this treatise and blocked its approval in the Council of the Indies and in the Council of Castile, as well as its approval by Salamancan theologians. Clayton, *Bartolomé de Las Casas*, 225, 350–52.

33. Pérez Fernández, *Cronología*, 761–62, 766; Pérez Fernández, *Fray Toribio Motolinía*, 144.

34. Las Casas, *Avisos y reglas*, in *Obras escogidas*, 5:239.

1548 to charge Las Casas with *lèse majesté* (high treason) and heresy.[35] Sepúlveda alleged that the king's authority to grant encomiendas and to allow slavery was being questioned, as well as the sovereign's right to dominium. He further alleged that it was heretical to deny the pope's power to donate the Indies to the Spanish kings.[36] Others, such as Chiapa's demoted cathedral dean (Gil de Quintana) and the wealthy encomendero (Baltasar Guerra), also condemned the seventh rule's seeming negation of the *señorio* (sovereignty) of the Spanish kings.[37]

Meanwhile, as a strictly moral question became a political matter, the bishop of Chiapa proceeded to defend himself on the charges of both treason and heresy in a treatise titled *Aquí se contienen treynta proposiciones muy jurídicas: En la quales sumaria y succintamente se toca[n] muchas cosas pertenecie[n]tes al derecho q[ue] la yglesia y los principes christianos tienen, o puede[n] tener sobre los infieles de qual quier especie que sean* (Here is contained thirty very juridical propositions which summarily and succinctly touch on many things pertaining to the right that the church and Christian princes have, or are able to have, over infidels of whatever type they may be).[38] In this text of thirty very juridical propositions, which was written in 1548 and/or 1549, Las Casas clarified rule 7 primarily in the seventeenth and eighteenth propositions. In the seventeenth proposition, he declared that the Spanish kings were authentic sovereigns of the Indies and supreme and universal rulers. In the eighteenth proposition, he argued that this supreme and universal sovereignty does not nullify the authority of the legitimate indigenous rulers in their nations and that their lordships are of a different type.[39] He showed

35. *Lèse majesté* refers to injury to the dignity of the monarch. Sepúlveda's charges surfaced in the same year that Las Casas urged the University of Salamanca to oppose Sepúlveda's publishing and also to solicit a ban on the publication of Sepúlveda's *Democrates secundus*. See Pinelo, *Epitome de la bibliotheca*, 58. However, it is not clear who denounced Las Casas before the Inquisition; Clayton opines that it was probably Sepúlveda; see *Bartolomé de Las Casas*, 145.

36. Fabié, *Vida y escritos*, 1:306–10; Losada, "Controversy," in Friede and Keen, *Bartolomé de Las Casas*, 255–60; Beckjord, *Territories of History*, 100.

37. Iglesias Ortega recounts how copies of the *Doce reglas* "flew directly from Chiapa to the royal Council"; see his *Bartolomé de Las Casas*, 526–27.

38. Las Casas, *Treynta proposiciones muy jurídicas*, in *Obras escogidas*, 5:249–57. For commentaries on this treatise, see Fabié, *Vida y escritos*, 1:311; Fernández Rodríguez, *Dominicos en el contexto*, 214; Iglesias Ortega, *Bartolomé de Las Casas*, 535; and G. Gutiérrez, *Las Casas*, 369–70, 385, 590nn19–20.

39. Las Casas, *Treynta proposiciones*, in *Obras escogidas*, 5:253.

how the titles granted by the pope to the Catholic monarchs, along
with the mandate to preach the gospel to the indigenous inhabitants
of the Indies and to care for their temporal and spiritual welfare,
in no way unseats the indigenous rulers and princes of the Indies.

After his succinct rebuttal of the charges made about his treatment of sovereignty, the bishop of Chiapa penned another eminently
juridical treatise to further nuance and amplify his position in the
seventeenth and eighteenth propositions of the *Treynta proposiciones muy jurídicas*. In a lengthy and cogent treatise titled *Tratado
comprobatorio del imperio soberano y principado universal que los
reyes de Castilla y León tienen sobre las Indias* (Treatise proving the
sovereign empire and universal principate that the kings of Castile
and Leon have over the Indies), he explicated the rights of Christian
princes and of the church over infidels and, by implication, over the
indigenous peoples.[40] In the proofs he gave in this *Tratado comprobatorio*, he drew extensively from Aristotle, from Thomas Aquinas's
Summa theologica (2a, q. 44, art. 1) and *Contra gentiles* (bk. 4, c. 74),
and from Peter Lombard's *Sentencias* (dist 24, art. 2, q. 1), as well as
copiously from canon law.[41] He explained how the pope holds temporal power solely as a means to a spiritual end, but not as direct or
directive authority. In the case of the indigenous infidels, the pope has
the obligation to guide them on the road to eternal life because they
are members *in potentia* and *in actu* of the body of Christ.[42] This
guidance must be by peaceful and persuasive preaching of the gospel.

40. Las Casas, *Tratado comprobatorio*, in *Obras completas*, 10:395–543. For commentaries about this treatise, see Fabié, *Vida y escritos*, 1:317; and G. Gutiérrez, *Las
Casas*, 369–75, 378, 387–88.

41. See, for example, Las Casas's *Tratado comprobatorio*, in *Obras completas*,
10:410.

42. In his debate at Valladolid, Las Casas defended the indigenous peoples by
arguing that they belonged to the category of unbelievers who were guiltless and
"innocent" because their ignorance was invincible and nonculpable. Therefore,
he maintained that they could not be condemned nor punished by human law or the
church. Indeed, he repeatedly insisted that only God could judge them. Las Casas,
Defense of the Indians, 54–79, 82, 84–86, 127–30, 137, 140, 154, 157–58, 186, 195–96,
l98. Moreover, Las Casas concurred with Aquinas's teaching that Christians were
incorporated *in actu* as members of the visible body of Christ by explicit faith and baptism and that, by divine law, nonbelievers and the nonbaptized (such as the indigenous
peoples) were incorporated as members of this visible body of Christ only *in potentia*
and, as such, the church still did not have jurisdiction over them. The possibility of
infidels becoming actual members of the church was also dependent, first, on Christ's
power as head of all people to save humankind and on Christ's grace, "which is more

Meanwhile, Sepúlveda had also notified the future Philip II about Las Casas's "scandalous and diabolic" *Confesionario*.[43] This letter may have precipitated the proposal by the Council of the Indies and the subsequent order from the emperor that a special junta be convened of "theologians, jurists, and scholars meeting concurrently with the Council of the Indies" to discuss and determine whether the "wars against the Indians were just and at least constituted a necessary preliminary to their Christianization."[44] Las Casas and Sepúlveda debated this issue in the junta's two sessions that took place in the chapel of San Gregorio in August 1550 and in May and June 1551. On the one hand, this debate in Valladolid constituted the climax of Las Casas's defense against the charges of treason and heresy, as he utilized legal theory and canon law to counter and undercut Sepúlveda's arguments that Las Casas's opponent drew from Aristotelian social philosophy and anthropology.[45] On the other hand, this

---

than sufficient to save all of the people of the world" and, second, as will be explicated later, "on the liberty and exercise of free will" in accord with the capabilities of all rational creatures. See Aquinas, *Summa theologica* 3a, q. 8, art. 3, reply to objection 1, art. 5; and Las Casas, *Tratado comprobatorio*, in *Obras completas*, 10:353a. About the influence of grace on inclinations to do good and on the exercise of humans' free will, see Aquinas, *Quaestiones disputatae de veritate*, 3a, q. 22, art. 8.

However, Las Casas went beyond the Thomistic teaching undergirding the Christological pathway to eternal life when he proposed in his *Tratado comprobatorio* that "it can also be said that Christ is head of infidels *in actu*." See *Obras escogidas*, 5:353a. Las Casas based this assertion on Christian teachings about the invisible workings of Christ's salvific grace in all people. Las Casas first distinguished *in actu* and *in potencia* in the 1543 "Memorial de Fray Bartolomé de Las Casas y Fray Rodrigo de Andrada al Rey" (in *Obras escogidas*, 5:192a). He further explicated this distinction in his controversy with Sepúlveda, wherein he argued that unbelievers who "don't acknowledge Christ or obey his commandments are not actually subject to him, that is, as regards their actions, but only potentially." Las Casas, *Defense of the Indians*, 56; see also Orique, "To Heaven or Hell"; and G. Gutiérrez, *Las Casas*, 255–56.

43. Friede, "Las Casas and Indigenism," in Friede and Keen, *Bartolomé de Las Casas*, 189.

44. Clayton, *Bartolomé de Las Casas*, 353; Hanke, *All Mankind Is One*, 62.

45. Adorno, *Polemics of Possession*, 71. On the first day of the junta in August 1550, Sepúlveda delivered a three-hour summary of the doctrine of his *Democrates secundus* to argue for the justice of the conquests. For the next five days, Las Casas read his rebuttal (word for word)—a five-hundred-page *Apología* (defense) titled in English as *In Defense of the Indians: The Defense of the Most Reverend Lord, Don Fray Bartolomé de Las Casas, of the Order of Preachers, Late Bishop of Chiapa, Against the Persecutors and Slanderers of the Peoples of the New World Discovered Across the Seas*. The summary, written at the end of the August session, included Sepúlveda's response to twelve arguments in Las Casas's rebuttal. Consequently, in the

debate gave Las Casas the opportunity to write, as he noted, a "special treatise" titled *Aquí se contiene una disputa o controversia* (Here is contained a dispute or controversy), in which he twice addressed the *Confesionario*. First, he established that Sepúlveda erred in *los hechos* (the facts) about the "evils and harm" done to the indigenous peoples. Las Casas asserted his own "thirty-five years" of eyewitness experience as evidence and source of his factual knowledge. Next, he pointed out that his *Confesionario* sought a total remedy for these "evils and harm" and reiterated that six theologians had approved his complete *Confesionario*. Then Las Casas established that Sepúlveda erred in *el derecho* (the law), and toward the "end" of upholding the law, Las Casas said, "compuse mi *Confesionario*" (I composed my confessionary).[46]

Although the special junta from 1550 to 1551 arrived at no conclusions, the Crown continued to support Las Casas's efforts on behalf of the indigenous people by its reaffirmation of existing protective legislation and by its promulgation of new legal safeguards.[47] For example, the Crown reissued past directives about the loads carried on the indigenous workers' backs and the age limit for such carriers. As in 1549, new regulations prohibited forcing workers to carry provisions to the mines or to urban centers. A later law obligated payment to workers who were constructing churches. In 1550 other laws ensued, as Las Casas's objectives provoked new practices and perspectives. As a result, the beginning of the 1550s generated increasing hostility on the part of the encomendero elite and colonial civil authorities, as well as overt friction between bishops and friars.[48]

The early 1550s also gave Las Casas time to begin devoting the remaining sixteen-plus years of his life to writing, publishing, and defending his understandings of the facts (*los hechos*) and of the law (*el derecho*) as applied to the Indies. Accordingly, in 1552 and 1553

---

next session, during two months of spring in 1551, the bishop of Chiapa again engaged in another lengthy and forceful rebuttal of Sepúlveda's replies, as recorded in his *Aquí se contiene una disputa o controversia* (in *Obras escogidas*, 5:293–348). See Hanke, *All Mankind Is One*, 68. For more details about the "Great Debate," see Clayton, *Bartolomé de Las Casas*, 342–86; Losada, "Controversy," in Friede and Keen, *Bartolomé de Las Casas*, 279–309, and the introduction to Las Casas, *Defense of the Indians*, 11–16.

46. Las Casas, *Avisos y reglas*, in *Obras escogidas*, 5:344b, 347ab, 348b.

47. Giménez Fernández, "Fray Bartolomé," 110.

48. Friede, "Las Casas and Indigenism," in Friede and Keen, *Bartolomé de Las Casas*, 193–95.

the now-retired bishop of Chiapa published a series of eight treatises, commonly referred to as the "Sevillian Cycle." These works, originally handwritten between 1541 and 1552, contained the best of his juridical-philosophical-theological thought.

One of these publications was the *Confesionario*. Each of the remaining seven treatises also contributed in some way to deeper understanding of the *Confesionario*, either by providing the facts or laws attendant to a particular issue or by containing direct references to the confessionary manual. For example, in his *Brevísima relación*, Las Casas detailedly described the horrific results (*hechos*) of the conquests—kingdom by kingdom—and of the encomienda grants and rigorously condemned the evils and harms done to the indigenous people by the Spanish encomenderos, conquistadors, and other colonial officials as violations of divine, natural, and human law. As such, this *Very Brief Account* provided an all-encompassing, factual scenario on which to base the need for restitution in the *Confesionario*.

Two of Las Casas's 1552 publications addressed the issues of the encomienda and slavery: these were *Entre los remedios* (Among the remedies) and *Sobre . . . los Indios que se han hecho en ellas esclavos* (Concerning Indians who have been made slaves); the *Confesionario* also obligated setting slaves free and making restitution. Significantly, the epigraph of the *Se han hecho en ellas esclavos* treatise not only contains the word *restitution* but "contains many reasons and juridical authorities to help the reader determine doubtful questions about restitution."[49]

Two other treatises included in the Sevillian Cycle of publications were those specifically written to clarify rule 7 of the *Doce reglas*: *Treynta proposiciones muy jurídicas* and *Tratado comprobatorio del imperio soberano*. As previously stated, these two treatises explicated

49. Fabié, *Vida y escritos*, 1:223. The epigraph reads, "Este es un tratado que el obispo de la Ciudad-Real de Chiapa, D. Fray Bartolomé de las Casas o Casaus, compuso por comisión del Consejo de las Indias sobre la material de los indios que se han hecho en ellas esclavos; el qual contiene muchas razones y autoridades juriídicas que pueden aprovochar a los lectores para determiner muchas y diversas cuestiones dudosas en material de restitucion y de otras que al presente los hombres el tiempo de agora tratan." (This is a treatise that the bishop of the Ciudad-Real of Chiapa [that] don fray Bartolomé de Las Casas or Casaus, commissioned to compose about the matter of the Indians who have been made slaves; in which is contained many reasons and juridical authorities that will benefit the readers in order to determine many diverse and doubtful questions concerning restitution and others dealt with now.)

and confirmed the Spanish monarch's titles and imperial sovereignty as well as the sovereignty of indigenous lords; they also upheld the papal mandate to solely Christianize and condemned the injustice of all armed conquests and forced conversion. In his *Una disputa o controversia*, Las Casas focused on one of the premises of the *Confesionario*: the injustice of all the wars of conquest. In an additional treatise, *Principia quaedam* (Certain principles), Las Casas further explicated the limitations of royal power and public law, as well as championed human freedom and the rights of indigenous people—considerations also implied in his *Avisos y reglas* for confessors.

Publication not only generated the diffusion of ideas and "reached a much wider circle" than did manuscripts but also made writings accessible to all.[50] The magnitude of a publication's circulation might also be calculated by the reactions it provoked.[51] Both kinds of consequences resulted with the publication of the *Confesionario*. In part because the manual was distributed gratuitously, the printed version surely reached beyond the friars who would have carried it to the Indies. Additionally, the printed treatise was "small"—a brief document consisting of sixteen folios, all written in third-person narrative. The introductory *Argumento* and the *Doce reglas* comprised fifteen pages; the *Adición de la primera y quinta reglas* (Appendix to the first and the fifth rules)—encompassed another fifteen pages. A shipment of this very succinct but highly polemical treatise accompanied the missionary friars who journeyed from Sanlúcar, Spain, to the Indies in November of that same year.[52]

50. Friede, "Las Casas and Indigenism," in Friede and Keen, *Bartolomé de Las Casas*, 191–92.

51. A. Gutiérrez, "Confesionario."

52. The initial plan was to leave Spain in September, but navigation issues postponed their departure for two months. Lorenzo Galmés, O.P., "Nota introductoria," in Las Casas, *Obras completas*, 10:365.

3

"I Guarantee . . .": A Passage to Heaven or a Ticket to Hell

An Analytic Commentary on the Text of the *Confesionario*

In characteristic Lascasian style, as the ink dried on the title page of his augmented and completed manuscript and immortalized the 1552 printed text, the content of his treatise emerged and was succinctly stated:

> *Aquí se contienen unos avisos y reglas para los confesores que oyeren confesiones de los españoles que son o han sido en cargo a los indios de las Indias del mar Océano, colegidas por el obispo de Chiapa don fray Bartolomé de Las Casas o Casaus, de la orden de Sancto Domingo.*

> Here are contained some advice and rules for confessors who might hear the confessions of the Spaniards who are or have been in charge of the Indians of the Indies of the sea Océano, compiled by the bishop of Chiapa, don friar Bartolomé de Las Casas or Casaus, of the Order of Saint Dominic.

To better understand Las Casas's advice and rules for confession, this commentary first presents certain distinctive features of his treatise, which reflected ancient as well as medieval patterns and approaches to the sacrament of confession.[1] For example, in keeping with the

---

1. To aid the reader in finding important passages as well as understanding significant points, this chapter of commentary employs the paragraph numbers in

genre of pastoral literature developed during the thirteenth and fourteenth centuries, the *Confesionario* resembles a *Summa confessorum* (Summary for confessors) insofar as it presents a juridical-theological understanding for confessors, especially in its *Adición*, which "incorporated opinions of theologians (such as Thomas Aquinas and other Dominicans) in his solutions" as well as "canon law, papal and conciliar legislation and the experience of pastoral authorities."[2] The *Confesionario* is also in part like the medieval *Confessionale* insofar as it contains case-by-case detailed and all-encompassing advice and rules for confessors.[3] This twofold eminently theoretical and meaningfully practical approach to cases of conscience also reflects Las Casas's use of the medieval casuistic style of argumentation in his attention to individual cases and their peculiarities.[4]

Preeminently distinctive is the public dimension attached to the confessions of guilty Spaniards. Just as in late medieval times, when communal rites of spiritual cleansing extended confessions into the public sphere, so too the juridical procedure required in the *Confesionario* constituted a public dimension in the otherwise private individual confessions of the conquerors, colonizers, and others responsible for the evils and harms done. The *Confesionario* required them to publicly pledge to make restitution in the presence of a scribe or notary of "suitable witnesses" (*Adición*, para. 55). This distinctive approach also drew on a long-standing medieval tradition of requiring restitution (for certain sins) prior to absolution.[5]

While these features contextualized the *Confesionario* in earlier traditions, Las Casas's treatise also comprehensively took into account the contemporary situation. For example, his confessionary condemns the crimes against humanity committed by the Spaniards in their conquests, exploitation, and enslavement of the indigenous peoples rather than the usual sins of the flesh, usury, arson and so forth. His *Confesionario* also addresses the old perennial Atlantic

---

parentheses that correspond to the paragraphs in the translated manuscript of the *Confesionario*.

2. Tentler, "Summa for Confessors," in Trinkaus and Oberman, *Pursuit of Holiness*, 103–4.

3. A. Gutiérrez, "Confesionario," 252.

4. Owensby, "Theater of Conscience," in Duve and Pihlajamaki, *New Horizons*, 126–27, 132–35.

5. Lea, *History of Auricular Confession*, 1:53–55, 65.

World moral issues of theft, slavery, and just war, which in the context of the Americas constituted significant early modern challenges. Indeed, his *Adición* constitutes an avalanche of juridical and theological citations to bolster his arguments about these crimes and other issues pertaining to cases of conscience.

Most significant, six discernible segments in the treatise frame his systematic response to the contemporaneous situation. These pertain to the requirement of the legal procedure, the assessment of guilt, the type of restitution, the components of confession, the obligations of confessors, and the Christian practice of temporal justice; these foci are elucidated in the subtitled segments of this commentary that now follows.

Argumento and Legal Procedure: All Hell Breaks Loose

The first segment of the *Confesionario* is prefaced by Las Casas's *Argumento*, in which he offered four contemporaneous reasons for writing the treatise as well as his qualifications to do so. First, as formerly stated, these rules to guide confessors in the forum of conscience were requested by some of his Dominican confreres. Second, these rules were written as a bishop's mandated response to the needs of his diocese. Third, some friars' reservations about rules 1 and 5 needed to be addressed. Last, Las Casas wanted to "prove manifestly," especially by his appended juridical assessment, that "there are cases in which the confessors are obliged from natural and divine precept [and canon law] to require those who confess to make a [suitable and juridical] pledge [to make restitution] before they are absolved" (para. 2). In the *Argumento*, in addition to citing his "long-service" and experience in the Indies, Las Casas also presented three additional sources of his authority. His episcopal position generated hierarchical validity. His Old Christian roots witnessed to his sanguineous legitimacy as indicated by his reference to his French surname "Casaus" to imply that he was not of Jewish or Muslim ancestry.[6] His theological credentials for this treatise were validated by six peninsular scholars.

---

6. In Spain, following the initiation of the Spanish Inquisition, especially during the sixteenth century, individuals went to great lengths to "prove" their so-called purity of blood—or their Old Christian status. See Hernández Franco, *Cultura y*

In his *Argumento*, Las Casas then referred to the confessors' obligations and, in the treatise's brief prologue and at the beginning of rule 1, ordered that his twelve rules be applied when confessors heard the confessions of conquistadors, encomenderos, and merchants (those bearing provisions to the conquerors) as well as of any others "who might have acquired part of their monies with and from Indians" (paras. 4, 5). In the rules he further specified and augmented the scope of those who must confess. Rules 1 to 6 of the *Doce reglas* pertained especially to cases of conscience involved in hearing the confessions of conquistadors; rules 7 and 8 of encomenderos; rule 9 of slave owners; rule 10 of married penitents; rule 11 of merchants, and rule 12 of those who might desire to involve themselves in future conquests or in the contemporaneous Peruvian rebellion. However, these categories of rules were not mutually exclusive, since directives within these rules were also generally applicable to all the categories of penitents who harmed the indigenous peoples (This was especially the case with rule 1.)

In the first segment of the *Confesionario*, Las Casas elucidated the obligatory legal procedure by first outlining the procedure in rule 1 of *Doce reglas*. Through this procedure Las Casas firmly linked the reception of the Sacrament of Penance and Reconciliation to the requirement of an initial solemn, public, and multifaceted legal

---

limpieza; and Kaplan, "Inception," in Aronson-Friedman and Kaplan, *Marginal Voices,* 19–41. Ironically, the 1506 Provincial Chapter of the Dominicans of Spain had issued a statute ordering that no one of Jewish descent was to receive the habit ("aliquem ad habitum nostrae religionis assumant, nec quem a genere judaeorum invenerit"). See de Heredia, "Estatuto ordenado por el Capítulo provincial dominicano de Burgos mandando que no se reciban el hábito a descendientes de raza judía—Burgos 16 de septiembre 1506," *Cartulario,* 3:262. However, at the beginning of his novitiate, Las Casas received the habit—apparently from Tomás de Berlanga, the prior of Santo Domingo. See Espinel, *San Esteban de Salamanca,* 69; and Remesal, *Historia general,* bk. 2, ch. 23. His novice master was also most likely Domingo Betanzos. See Pérez Fernández, *Bartolomé de Las Casas,* 64. If Las Casas were of Jewish ancestry, he was in good company—Hernando de Talavera, Francisco de Vitoria, and other prominent Spaniards shared this sanguineous heritage. Talavera, the archbishop of Granada, who opposed Cisneros's method of forced conversion of the Muslims of Granada, suffered the indignity of his family being investigated on the grounds of heretical associations relating to their Jewish ancestry. Furthermore, and perhaps in an effort to reinforce his case against possible and present detractors, Las Casas asserted his ancestry by referring to himself as an Old Christian. See Las Casas, "Carta al consejo de Indias" (April 30, 1534)," in *Obras escogidas,* 5:58b).

obligation to make restitution for the evils and harms done to the indigenous people. As previously stated, prior to confession, or at least before giving absolution, the confessor was obliged to ask the penitent for a legal pledge, which had to be sworn in the presence of a "public scribe" or notary "of the king" as a "public act," in which the penitent had to "declare, ordain and concede" certain "things"; the declarations of the penitent and the confessor were to be officially recorded by a scribe or notary (rule 1, paras. 5, 11).

The penitent's first declaration pertained to membership in the church. Alluding to the Spaniards' expected "faithful" adherence to the norms and doctrines of Christianity, Las Casas mandated that the offending Spaniards had to approach the sacrament with the desire (if they were dying, as referred to in rule 1) "to leave this life without offenses against God" because they wished "to appear before the divine judge in a secure state." Furthermore, if they were in good health (as addressed in rule 5), Las Casas reasoned that since the Spaniards had placed their eternal salvation in jeopardy by their atrocious sins against the indigenous people of the Indies, which surely must have weighed heavily on their consciences, receiving this sacrament would "unburden [their] conscience" (rule 1, para. 6).

The penitent's second declaration pertained to contracts in civil society. Las Casas obligated the offending Spaniard to give their confessor "complete power" (tantamount to an all-encompassing "power of attorney") over the penitent's assets in the form of a solemn pledge or other public obligation to make full restitution. That is, the penitent had to empower the confessor to distribute his properties and money, as well as to immediately free all slaves held (rule 1, para. 6).

After obtaining the appropriate legal pledge, Las Casas's procedure called for an assessment of guilt. This required the penitent to disclose, acknowledge, and take responsibility for his participation in the unjust conquests, colonization, captivity, and control of the indigenous people; the scribe put this information in writing. To aid in this process, Las Casas presented examples in rule 1 of Spaniards who had participated in the evils and harms done in the Indies, about which the penitent had to freely volunteer information, and the confessor had to thoroughly interrogate him to assess their guilt. The last civil and public element of the procedure required that the penitent revoke any previous wills or oaths and renounce "whatever laws that may help him contest [his pledge]." Accordingly, he took a "solemn oath" irrevocably renouncing any such previous wills and allocating all his liquid and fixed assets to the prescribed restitution (rule 1, paras. 7, 10–11).

Implicit in this oath was the provision that if the penitent reneged, his assets would be transferred and subjected to ecclesiastical jurisdiction. For several cases of conscience in the *Confesionario*, Las Casas judged that the penitent would also be obligated to give the same power (that was given to the priest) to the penitent's bishop and the ecclesiastical judiciary to "constrain or compel the penitent in the juridical ecclesiastical forum to all that was said above." There were also several cases that Las Casas noted were best handled by the bishop since the matter (such as excommunication) pertains to the prelate by canon law (rule 1, paras. 6, 11; rule 5, para. 17; rule 6, para. 19; *Adición*, para. 44).

Guilty Ones: Defining the Hell-Bent

In a second discernible segment of the *Confesionario*, Las Casas identified the astounding variety of guilty Spaniards who wanted or needed to confess, and from whom confessors were duty-bound to require the pledge of restitution. These included all those involved in the conquest as well as in the capturing, controlling, and commercializing of indigenous people. In the *Doce reglas* section of the treatise, Las Casas first focused on the conquistadors. He maintained that their guilt was twofold: they had engaged in "such and such conquests or wars against Indians in these Indies," and they were involved in the subsequent "robberies, violence, injuries, deaths, and any capture of Indians." He declared that the destruction that they wrought "in and throughout many villages and places" and in all the kingdoms of the indigenous world was "driven only by their great ambition and insatiable greed" (rule 1, para. 7; rule 2, para. 13). In his assessment of the conquistadors' guilt, Las Casas also implicated the merchants: "those who carried arms and merchandize to those who were conquering and making war on the Indians, thus [they too] engaged in bellicose actions"; they also were "participants and with others caused those evils, thefts and harms that were carried out with the help of the said arms" (rule 1, para. 5; rule 11, para. 37). For the bishop of Chiapa, no war fought in the Indies was a just war; he demonstrated this by references to the components of a just war.[7] In addition to his harsh stance against the unjust wars, Las Casas took a clear position on the legitimacy of indigenous sovereignty as well as on restitution and based this on his argument that all wars and gains were unlawful.[8] The activist-cleric later paid a price for his political stand: he was denounced for treason.

In his imputing of guilt, Las Casas then focused on the encomenderos—on the settlers who had indigenous people from apportionment or in encomiendas, as well as those who received tributes from the natives. His assessment of these settlers' guilt was also twofold. First, he contended that "throughout the Indies with the entrance of the Spaniards . . . , the subjection and servitude in which they might have put these people . . . [is] contrary to all natural law and the law of nations, and also against divine law; and therefore is entirely unjust, iniquitous, tyrannical, and deserving of all eternal fire and, consequently, null, invalid and without any value and weight of law." Second, he contended that those Spaniards also "have not fulfilled . . . the task . . . to preach to and to teach these people [the Christian faith]." He denounced their actions and activities as "against justice" and pointed out that they "robbed and possessed [the tribute taxes] by evil conduct." The worst offenders, for Las Casas, were the Spanish miners and ranchers; they were "most inhuman, cruel and soulless"; indeed, the bishop of Chiapa called them the "executioners" of indigenous peoples. According to Las Casas, the guilt of all these Spanish would-be penitents, as well as of the conquistadors, resided in the fact that these Spaniards did not bring any *hacienda* (wealth

7. In his judgment concerning the injustice of all the wars of conquest, Las Casas drew on Aquinas's theory of just war, as did the philosophers and theologians of the School of Salamanca or the Peninsular School. This theory enunciated three fundamental principles of just war: declaration by competent authority, just cause, and right intention. Additional principles of just war, which were espoused in the sixteenth century, included war as a last resort, protection of the innocent, proportionality, and the reasonable possibility of success. On the basis of these understandings of *ius gentium*, Las Casas concluded that the Spaniards' wars of conquest were condemnable as violations of the traditional principles of just war. For the development of the theory of just war, see Russell, *Just War*. To consider the subsequent application of just-war theory, see two of Johnson's works: *Limitation of War* and *Just War Tradition*.

8. Moreover, Adorno points out that after Las Casas returned to Spain in 1540, he made his most vigorous denunciation of unjust wars against the indigenous population. See *Polemics of Possession*, 74–76, 338n35.

and possessions) from Castilla; instead, all that they possessed in the Indies (except for profits from agriculture) was stolen from the indigenous peoples (rule 7, paras. 27, 28; rule 8, para. 32; rule 1, para. 8).

In like manner, slave owners were guilty—no matter the way indigenous people were made slaves, "or by whatever title they are held, possessed, purchased or obtained through inheritance, or also purchased from Indians, or received as tribute from villages of Indians." Voicing what Las Casas alleged was common knowledge, he charged "that in all the Indies, since they were discovered until today, there has not been one or another Indian who has been justly enslaved." Such was their grave sin (rule 9, para. 33).

Las Casas also ascribed collective guilt in his indictment that "there is no Spaniard in the Indies who may have acted in good faith" in the wars of conquest, in the transporting and kidnapping of the indigenous people, in the enslaving and selling of the native inhabitants, and in providing arms and merchandize for the conquerors. Indeed, Bishop Las Casas insisted that each was responsible not just for one's own sins but for those of others—not just for their private profit but for the benefits acquired by all; that is, the individual was culpable for "all the evils and harms that others did [or] with whom he collaborated; . . . every one of them is obliged *in solidum* [in joint liability]" (rule 1, para. 9; rule 2, para. 13).[9]

Indeed, Las Casas was poignantly aware of the personal and communal dimensions of the sins committed by the Spaniards in the Indies. Implicit in the sacrament, the dimensions of personal remorse for injustices committed and of communal restoration of indigenous rights and possessions were necessary. Accordingly, the bishop combined and concretized in practice these twofold dimensions of the sacrament with the spiritual dimension of healing their relationship with God and, in so doing, linked restitution to the spiritual dimension of eternal salvation—both of the Spaniards and of the indigenous people.

Las Casas's assessments of guilt also pertained to the Spaniards' role and duties as Christians. First, by his estimation, all the Spaniards impeded as well as never pursued the "final cause" of their presence in the Indies, that is, the evangelization, conversion, and (ultimately) the salvation of the indigenous inhabitants. Second,

9. Rivera-Pagán, *Violent Evangelization*, 318n12.

in his assessment of the Spaniards' having placed these peoples in "subjection and servitude" using every means and ends, Las Casas drew from moral theology and international law when he charged that all this has "been contrary to all natural law and the law of nations, and also against divine law" (rule 7, para. 28). He judged that the Spaniards violated the divine precepts to love God and one's neighbor, as well as natural law that demanded avoidance of evil and pursuit of the good. Furthermore, in his judgment, he pointed out that the Spaniards violated *ius gentium*, which protected the indigenous peoples as rational human beings and therefore as free and equal to all human persons and respected the freedom and equality of all nations (including those of the indigenous peoples). In this Las Casas utilized an ontological premise found in Greco-Roman antiquity and in canon law tradition: all humans and all nations are equal.[10] From the latter tradition, he drew on Gratian's second definition of natural law that "natural law is common to all nations because it exists everywhere through natural instinct, not because of any enactment."[11]

Restitution: Payback Time

In a third discernible segment of the *Confesionario*, after following the initial procedural steps and, as such, having presented the *Argumento* and defined the types of offenders and assessed their guilt, Las Casas then designated the process for determining the required restitution. While ideal restitution seemingly would achieve some level of adequate restoration or compensation, as stated in the *Argumento* and in rule 5, divine law and natural law, as well as canon law, obliged the confessor to withhold absolution from the offending Spanish penitents "unless first they might restore *all* that was stolen," even "the entire hacienda . . . without leaving anything for his heirs." The intended restitution was not meant as a kind of "universal expropriation"; rather, basing his judgments on "dogma that had been accepted

10. This ancient-medieval ideal, which also implied the common supernatural destiny of all people, came from Cicero, whom Las Casas directly quoted. See Las Casas, *Witness*, 174–76; and Phelan, "Apologetic History," 96.

11. For the definition of natural law, see Gratian, *Treatise on Laws*, dist. 1, c. 7.2.

for hundreds of years," the question for Las Casas was whether or not the restitution was appropriate in a particular case of conscience.[12] To determine this, and as explicated in the rules as well as in the cases of conscience addressed in the *Adición*, confessors were instructed to investigate and take inventory of the penitent's wealth, as well as to specify the different ways of making restitution based on the Spaniard's possessions and life circumstances (rule 3, para. 14; rule 4, para. 16; rule 5, para. 18; rule 6, para. 19).

For example, the restitution required of conquistadors included the restoration and repopulation of the villages and places they damaged or destroyed (rule 3, paras. 14, 15). Additionally, in Las Casas's application of the medieval dictum of Pope Eugene III, the conquistador must "restore all that was stolen" (rule 5, para. 18). In like manner, Las Casas applied Aquinas's principle that "ransacking in an unjust war, or even malicious stealing in a just battle, is a great sin that requires restitution of stolen goods."[13] Furthermore, the penitent conquistador had to swear to "never again conquer or make war against Indians" or to go to Peru during this time of its uprisings (rule 12, para. 38).[14] Concomitantly, merchants were required to pay back the monies that "they might have earned from the merchandize that they might have sold to [conquistadors;] even if [the merchants] might not have carried arms, they are obligated to pay restitution" (rule 11, para. 37).

The restitution required of slave owners was that "at once [they are] to grant [their slaves] irrevocable freedom, without any limitation or condition" (rule 1, para. 9) and to "pay them all they were owed for each year and month that their services and labors merited" (rule 9, para. 33). To make restitution for those slaves the Spaniard no longer held, the slave owner was obliged to purchase them back; if he did not have the money to do so, he was obliged to make himself a slave to free those he sold; if the slaves were deceased, he had to give the money for religious works and purposes.[15]

12. Wagner and Parish, *Life and Writings*, 167–68.

13. Aquinas, *Summa theologica*, 2a–2ae, q. 66, art. 8; Rivera-Pagán, *Violent Evangelization*, 252.

14. For a classic study about the Spaniards who conquered Peru as well as the early colonial period, see Lockhart's *Men of Cajamarca* and *Spanish Peru*. For an excellent source about the conquest of Peru as well as the conquest in general, see Restall's *Seven Myths*.

15. Las Casas qualified his order, however, by contending that "if someone should be considered truly a slave or taken in wars that the Indians had among themselves

The restitution required of encomenderos, whom Las Casas persistently referred to as "settlers" and in which population cohort he included miners and ranchers, consisted of the amount they took in services and tributes. He particularly called for rigorous assessments and restitution of the tributes, which he contended were taken "unjustly, excessively, and tyrannically." He contended that these Spaniards were, "for many and juridical reasons" (rule 7, paras. 27, 28), also obliged to make restitution for all the profit and possessions they had acquired. Since these encomenderos came to the Indies with nothing, they must stay in or leave the Indies with nothing: they must restitute all. Moreover, Las Casas held that "in the case that the aggrieved and their heirs all are dead, [the confessor] might command that part of the satisfaction might be that [the penitent] resolve to remain in the land the rest of his life . . . to give him something more than the necessary goods that might have been restored" (rule 6, para. 26).[16]

Variations existed in the amounts and kinds of restitution that Las Casas assigned in the *Doce reglas* and ascribed in the cases of conscience found in the *Adición*. For example, because the merchants allegedly excelled in *mala fe* (bad faith), Las Casas rigorously demanded full-monetary restitution from them, whereas healthy but poor Spaniards could make restitution by their labors, including by teaching Christian doctrine. Social class-related exceptions were made for poor Spaniards (especially virtuous ones); those with no revenue would not be obliged to pay the restitution owed from the conquests, yet those of noble blood would be reduced to poverty or, at best, be given a "modest sustenance." Some could also keep income from nonindigenous sources. While nothing except alms would be given to the Spaniards' legitimate children, in other circumstances, provision was sometimes made for widows and children (rule 6, paras. 19, 20). Ever attentive to the law, Las Casas also recognized women's rights to property and to own slaves (rule 10, para. 35).[17]

---

or by their just laws, then what I am saying is not understood concerning such a one" (rule 9, para. 33).

16. Seemingly, Las Casas means that the penitent can make partial restitution by peacefully populating and humbly working the land.

17. Here Las Casas is speaking of women; as such, this prompts one to think of future scholarship related to extracting a gender reading of his work.

Healing Relationships: To Hell and Back

In a fourth discernible segment of the *Confesionario*, Las Casas's Christian worldview, bolstered by his fidelity to the tradition of private confession and in addition to the importance of restitution, focused on the healing of relationships with God and with others by recourse to the three components or acts of penitence in the sacrament as a framework. The first component of the matter of confession, that is, contrition, was especially reflected in rule 1 of the *Doce reglas*, where he addressed the need for forgiveness and for sorrow at both the end of the designated procedure and the start of the sacramental rite.[18] For example, Las Casas required the penitent[s] to ask for pardon from the indigenous people "for the injury they did to them in making them slaves, usurping their liberty . . . or . . . for having purchased, possessed and served himself with them in bad faith" (rule 1, para. 9). The Dominican bishop contended that this conciliatory gesture gave the indigenous inhabitants an opportunity to "voluntarily and graciously . . . remit to them [the tribute] and pardon [the Spaniard]" and thus "exercise charity" (rule 8, para. 31). Indeed, central to Christian thinking, and also drawing from Jewish theological understanding, was the issue of forgiveness and the need for reconciliation (when possible) between the offended and the offender. In the case of the Sacrament of Penance and Reconciliation, the offenders (in addition to making restitution or satisfaction) were seeking personal reconciliation with God and with the Christian community (the church), that is, forgiveness. Yet this process of forgiveness also required public expression to heal the wrong done to the offended, that is, reconciliation. Such forgiveness and reconciliation created a *metanoia*—a change of heart.[19] Essential to this *metanoia* was the obligation asserted by Las Casas in the *Confesionario* that the penitent must "lament for all those they offended" by his sin, as well

18. After the priest greets the penitent, the basic rite of confession is as follows: both priest and penitent make the sign of the cross; the priest listens to (and, if appropriate, asks about) committed sins; the priest proffers a penance; the penitent offers a prayer of contrition; the priest says the words of absolution; and the priest invites the penitent to go in peace.

19. For the case of this discussion, in New Testament Greek *metanoia*/μετάνοια implies an alteration in the tendency and action of the entire inner nature of the person—a changed intellective, affective, and moral disposition.

as "lament all the days of his life for the great sin and harm he did to his neighbors" (rule 2, para. 13; rule 6, para. 24; rule 9, para. 34).

The second component of the matter of confession pertained to the actual confession of sins; penitents needed to declare and substantiate their guilt by telling the priest all the sins that they remembered. Las Casas charged that because of procrastination or "stubborn will" so many failed to do so, and consequently "year after year" the would-be penitent remained in mortal sin (*Adición*, para. 61). Echoing the teachings of Thomas de Vio Cajetan, Las Casas further reminded the confessors that none of the Spaniards could claim invincible ignorance, especially given that "everybody knows about the tyrannies, ravages and robberies they did": that they all sinned by their "lack of the fear of God and of eternal damnation" as well as by their *mala fe* (para. 66; rule 1, para. 9; rule 2, para. 13). Above all, they sinned "against the divine precept that commands us to love our neighbor"; as such, they were a "scandalous and disgraceful example of our holy Faith" (rule 8, para. 30; rule 12, para. 38).

The third component of the matter of confession pertained to restorative justice. Las Casas differentiated the types of restoration as restitution or satisfaction. Restitution meant "making whole again" what was taken unjustly. Satisfaction meant compensating for the injustice done when restitution was not possible (e.g., the person was dead, the resources were consumed, or the village was destroyed). The theologian-jurist declared that, if the penitent could not make restitution (as specified by the confessor), satisfaction (also as specified by the confessor) must be made for the evils and harms done. These two dimensions of restorative justice generated ethical and physical problems. Morally, for restorative justice to be carried out, the offenders needed to show remorse and to take responsibility by admitting guilt. Materially, when there was no way to make restitution, the offenders needed to make satisfaction for the wrong committed against the aggrieved, which was meant as a type of partial compensation for the irreparable injustice.[20] For example, penitents who are poor but healthy encomenderos or settlers could remain in

20. Las Casas understood material restitution as restoring or repairing of the physical damage done to the indigenous inhabitants—restoring what had been taken or repairing what had been damaged. Of course, as Las Casas pointed out, when this was not possible, some type of compensatory payment was required; that is satisfaction.

the Indies and "work [supporting the] teaching and indoctrinating by [members of the mendicant] religious [Orders]; and he personally . . . may teach and defend and provide for them [the indigenous people], and help and gain favor for them before magistrates and other persons and, finally, may he aid and assist them with their needs," that is, with the basic necessities of life (rule 8, para. 29). While only binding in conscience and not in law courts, the modes of satisfaction were generally limited and were geared to serving justice by avoidance of sin and by good works on behalf of the indigenous people.[21]

Confessors' Obligations: Come Hell or High Water

In a fifth discernible segment of the *Confesionario*, Las Casas offered several cases of conscience to demonstrate how the process of requiring restitution also levied great obligations on the confessor. In the *Adición* the bishop of Chiapa exhaustively and exhaustingly reiterated that, for the sake of justice for the indigenous people, the confessor's nonnegotiable duty was to elicit a legal pledge from the penitent to make restitution. Copiously applying the science of jurisprudence, Las Casas specifically made manifest the confessor's obligation in two cases of conscience that pertained to canon law, as well as presented four cases of conscience based on divine and natural law (paras. 40–50).

Citing canon law from the *Decretals* and referring the reader to John of Freiburg's *Summa confessorum*, Las Casas addressed the first case of conscience, which in medieval times applied to those who robbed, burned, or transgressed churches.[22] The various ways of proceeding were as follows. First, if the Spaniard had not made restitution or at least had not given legal assurance that he would do so, then he would be denied the Sacrament of Penance and, specifically, absolution. Second, if after a life of "contempt and hardness," the Spaniard repented and also made restitution or assured that this

21. Tentler, "Summa for Confessors," in Trinkaus and Oberman, *Pursuit of Holiness,* 121–22.
22. Las Casas posited other canon law–related cases of conscience about public moneylenders and the excommunicated but regarded these as irrelevant or as matters for the ecclesiastical judiciary and thus outside of the confessor's jurisdiction (rule 8, para. 29).

would be done, a canonical papal directive allowed him to be absolved of his sins and to receive the sacrament of the Eucharist. However, there was a penalty: he could not have a Christian burial. There was also a penalty for the confessor if he attended the funeral or accepted alms or had participated in the wrongdoings. Third, if the Spaniard did not want to make restitution nor to assure that restitution would be done, and the confessor absolved the penitent anyway—no matter whether the penitent was healthy or dying—the confessor would be punished for absolving the penitent, for conducting the burial, or for accepting alms, by being laicized and stripped of all ecclesiastical benefits (*Adición*, paras. 41–44).

Referencing divine law to love God and one's neighbor and natural law to avoid evil and pursue the good and to give others their due, Las Casas also informed confessors how their role as counselors and spiritual judges, as well as their public office in church and society, obliged them to ask for a "suitable and sufficient" pledge to make restitution from the penitent. Accordingly, as a counselor, the confessor must by "divine and natural law . . . provide the penitent in counsel and admonition and mandate all that is suitable for the good and security of the [penitent's] conscience." As spiritual judge "placed by God in his universal Church" and therefore responsible for the "health of the suffering soul," the confessor, as Las Casas pointed out, was obligated to "judge justly . . . to practice justice" (paras. 45–47).

Las Casas stated, however, three cases in which the "deserving and dispossessed may not be able to obtain justice" unless the confessor had asked for and received a sure pledge from the penitent. One case concerned the size of the debt, which for encomenderos would be very large and numerous and thus might make complete repayment almost impossible. Two other cases appertained to the need to make vehement presumptions about the penitent.[23] One was about the penitent who frequented the sacrament but never complied with the pledge he made each time, but who (it was presumed) may do so in the future. The other was the case of a penitent who feared neither

23. In canon law, presumption has its place only when positive proofs are wanting, and yet the formulation of some judgment is necessary. Presumption is never in itself an absolute proof, as it only presumes that something is true. Presumption is called *vehement* when the probability is very strongly supported by most urgent conjectures.

God nor the courts as well as manifested "weak devotion" and about
whom it could be presumed that he would do little to carry out a
pledge. Besides these three cases of conscience, Las Casas offered a
fourth case in which the aggrieved may or do not receive a remedy,
that is, when there is a diversity of opinions, and when few of the
articulators had the education, expertise, and experience to judge
what was just (paras. 48–50, 59–60).

To effect a "sure pledge" as well as a "suitable and sufficient" one,
Las Casas spelled out different ways to secure restitution. The confessor might legally bind the penitent to make deposits, establish a
deadline, or furnish a credible guarantee for the required restitution.
In other cases of conscience—except for the confessions of conquistadores, another option was available: a *juratoria* pledge (promissory
oath) may be made, but only if the penitent could not be constrained
to make suitable and sufficient deposits or guarantees or public obligation. These options would at least fulfill the confessor's duty to ask
for the required oath (paras. 45, 54–58).

Las Casas also pointed out that some aspects of cases of conscience
could be handled by the exterior forums of ecclesiastical and secular
judiciaries.[24] He warned confessors, however, that the public good—
which, along with aid to the defenseless (read indigenous peoples),
was the responsibility of these judiciaries—might not be served.
In this situation, he blamed the blindness and hypocrisy of secular
justices, and he decried their ignorance of and disregard for canon law
(paras. 53–55).

To compensate for secular irresponsibility, Las Casas presented
several different legal ways of obliging penitents to pledge restitution, which utilized the external ecclesiastical forum. For example,
the confessor could ask for a pledge "on behalf of another," which is
called stipulation.[25] Although a notary would not sign this type of

24. Ecclesiastical tribunals had their own executives, including *alguacils*, a kind of
episcopal marshal, to enforce their sentences. When they were unable to execute the
sentences of the judges of an ecclesiastical court, recourse had to be made to the secular
arm. Dutto, *Life of Bartolomé*, 466–67.

25. Roman civil law defined contracts as real (*re*), verbal (*verbis*), literal (*literis*),
or consensual (*consensu*). A real contract was one such as a loan or pledge, which was
not perfected until something had passed from one of the parties to the other. A verbal
contract or stipulation was perfected by a spoken formula, which consisted of a question
by one of the parties and an exact corresponding answer by the other (e.g., "Do you
agree or promise?" "I agree" or "I promise"). Canonical and moralist doctrine on the

pledge, the "deserving dispossessed party" could have recourse to
the external forum and approach a magistrate to demand payment.
Furthermore, like tacit pledges, stipulation also bound the heirs to
payment. However, if the penitent was alive, he too would pay the
amount designated for restitution in the external forum (paras. 44,
51–52).

However, if the external forum failed, Las Casas was convinced
that justice could be obtained through the Sacrament of Penance and
Reconciliation—which, as he so frequently stressed throughout his
Confesionario, would ensure justice for the wronged and unburden
the conscience of the penitent. The wronged would receive what is
their due. Yet he forcefully warned the confessors that their failure to
"complete or badly complete their spiritual and public offices" would
precipitate great damage: (1) to the penitent, whose confessions
would be insincere or inadequate; (2) to the indigenous peoples, for
whom the confessor would not be able to offer a remedy; and (3) to
the cleric himself, whose consequent mortal sin(s) merited eternal
hell fire (paras. 61–63).

Then, likening the confessor to Ezekiel's "watchman of Israel"—
on duty as sentinel and sentry—the last advice given by the aging
bishop of Chiapa to the confessors was not to "aggrieve" the penitent nor to "oblige him . . . where he is not obliged" (paras. 66–67).
Indeed, as noted previously, Bishop Bartolomé likened these confessors to physicians whose task was to heal, and "to underscore the
fact that no matter how harsh the penance, its purpose was medicinal
rather than penal."[26]

Christian Temporal Justice and Restitution: Snatched from the Fires of Hell

In a sixth discernible segment of the *Confesionario*, Las Casas's advice
and rules for confessors included a twofold interweaving of justice
with Christian behavior. First, he understood the exercise of religion
as fundamentally doing good deeds and, as such, emphasized Christian

---

subject of stipulation developed from Roman civil law, whose rigid formalism was tem-
pered and replaced by moral theology as the science of Christian behavior. Stipulation,
which could be upheld in church courts, was adopted into canon law.

26. Favazza, *Order of Penitents*, 123, 123n5; García-Morato-Soto, "Necesidad de la
confesión," 277.

practice. Second, he asserted that fundamental to the practice of the faith meant giving others their due—to act justly with respect to the wronged and dispossessed indigenous people, to make restitution.

This intransigent and lifelong preoccupation with temporal justice canopied Las Casas's focus on restitution in the *Confesionario*. Drawing from Thomistic theology, the Dominican bishop held that justice directed humans in their relations with others as equals and did so in two ways: as a virtue requiring personal commitment to habitually rendering to others their due and as an objective moral order demanding conformity to what was "right." The guilty Spaniards did neither. Furthermore, according to Aquinas, God established an order of justice (i.e., eternal law or divine Providence) and endowed all creatures with what was proper to their different natures.[27] As creatures whose nature was rational, free, and social, humans were to act in their relations with others in accord with this established order of eternal law: they were to render to others their due. That is, in accord with the divine structuring of right relationships among humans as equals, humans were to do what was objectively "right" (moral) or, as Las Casas (and Aquinas) stated, the "just thing."[28]

At the level of personal conduct, Las Casas would have understood justice in general as the highest of the cardinal virtues (the others being prudence, temperance, fortitude); this virtue he found grossly lacking in the offending Spaniards.[29] At the level of communal behavior, commutative justice, which concerns relations with others, requires that restitution be made whenever the virtue of justice or the moral order has been violated. As such, according to moral theology, restitution is an act of commutative justice that gives to others their due by restoring a certain balance or equilibrium to repair injury done.

In the case of Las Casas's *Confesionario*, this restorative justice meant making right the wrong that was done. Accordingly,

27. Aquinas, *Summa theologica*, 1a, q. 21, arts. 1–2; 2a–2ae, q. 57, art. 1; 2a–2ae, q. 58, art. 1; 1a, q. 21, arts. 1–2. Aquinas's theology built on Aristotle's principle of justice, which was an objectively right state of affairs in a particular context; that is, an objective order of right was something inherent in the nature of a situation. Tierney, *Idea of Natural Rights*, 21.

28. Aquinas, *Summa theologica*, 2a–2ae, q. 57, 58, art. 1. Justice, as a virtue (as well as over and above other virtues) had its own special proper object: the "right."

29. For a discussion of Aquinas's views on the cardinal virtues, see Floyd, "Thomas Aquinas."

Las Casas labored so that the indigenous people would receive justice; he demanded that the Spanish penitents do justice by making restitution or satisfaction and charged confessors to exercise justice by requiring legal pledges and by judging justly. In restorative justice the victims, that is, the indigenous people, were central to the process. The focus was to repair the harm done to the victims and, in the process, to perhaps heal the offenders and the wider community.[30]

In summary, restitution (and at least satisfaction) was required for the sake of justice. Indeed, justice was the motivating factor in Las Casas's vision for the peaceful evangelization of the indigenous peoples as well as for the eternal salvation of indigenous people and Spaniards alike, and restitution was the necessary "total remedy" demanded of the Spanish Christians—one that Las Casas sought since 1514. Toward these ends the bishop of Chiapa placed restitution at the heart of the Sacrament of Penance and Reconciliation and at the center of his *Confesionario*. Las Casas penned this emblematic treatise at the height of his intellectual maturity and experiential expertise, as well as from the core of his episcopal practice, prophetic message, and philosophical-theological-canonistic writings, as he— the jurist—battled for justice for the indigenous people.[31]

Las Casas left this rich legacy to his mendicant confreres. While his *Confesionario* gained decided support from the Franciscans and Dominicans in New Spain from 1546 onward, among the mendicant missionaries in Peru sociopolitical, socioeconomic, and ethical dissension of opinion about the treatise continued. In 1560, however, because of alterations to encomiendas and because of assumptions about the moral correctness of this colonial system (as long as encomenderos scrupulously "cared" for the welfare of their indigenous workers), a confessionary titled *Sobre las obligaciones de los conquistadores* was published in Lima. This publication reflected unyielding Lascasian demands for restitution on the part of conquistadors, merchants, and servants of conquistadors. The following ecclesiastical and civil leaders spoke from firsthand experience in the Andes and signed the document: Gerónimo de Loaysa (the archbishop of Lima and the master general of the Dominican Order); Gaspar de Carvajal

30. Daly, "Revisiting the Relationship," in Strang and Braithwaite, *Restorative Justice*, 36.
31. Cantú, "Evoluzione e significato."

(the Dominican provincial and theologian); Francisco de Morales (the Franciscan provincial and local prior); the superior of the Mercedarians in Lima; two Augustinian friars, including their provincial and a *letrado*; and, seemingly, the lawyer for the Lima Audiencia.[32]

To facilitate understanding of the legacy of Las Casas's sixteenth-century *Confesionario* for contemporary scholars, the first complete, edited, annotated, and glossed English translation of the bishop of Chiapa's significant and influential treatise—*Aquí se contienen unos avisos y reglas para los confesores que oyeren confesiones de los españoles que son o han sido en cargo a los indios de las Indias del mar Océano, colegidas por el obispo de Chiapa don fray Bartolomé de Las Casas o Casaus, de la orden de Sancto Domingo*—is now presented.

32. Tibesar, "Documents."

English Translation

Here are contained some advice and rules for confessors who might hear the confessions of the Spaniards who are or have been in charge of the Indians of the Indies of the sea Océano, compiled by the bishop of Chiapa, don friar Bartolomé de las Casas or Casaus, of the Order of Saint Dominic.[1]

The Reason for the Present Tract

[1] Some religious of the Order of Saint Dominic, with zeal and desire to aid the souls of Spaniards who are in the Indies, especially in confessions, yet without prejudice to their own [souls], have a few times pleaded with and charged the bishop of Chiapa, don fray Bartolomé de Las Casas or Casaus, friar of the same Order, as long-serving and very experienced in the things that have happened in those lands, that he might give them some rules by which they might

---

1. This first complete translation has endeavored to balance fidelity to the original text with readability. Unless otherwise stated, the following footnotes are the translator's own. Comments by Arturo Bernal y Palacios, O.P., are followed by [ABP]; notes followed by [BLC, *Avisos*] derive from Las Casas, *Avisos y reglas*, in *Obras completas*, 10:369–88. All paragraphs of the translation are sequentially numbered, and all words, phrases, and comments in brackets are added for clarity and are not part of the original manuscript.

¶ Argumento del pre/
sente tractado.

Algunos religiosos dla
orden de sancto Domingo: cõ zelo y desseo
de aprouechar enlas animas delos españo
les q están enlas yndias: especialmête enlas
cõfessiones / pero sin perjuyzio delas proprias: rogarõ
y encargarõ algûas vezes al obispo de Chiapa dõ fray
Bartholome delas casas/o casaus frayle dla misma or-
dê: como psona biê antigua y enlas cosas passadas en
aquellas tierras muy expertimentada: q les diesse algu
nas reglas: por las qles se pudiessen guiar enel foro de
la consciencia: porq assi mismo no dañassen y a los pe-
nitentes aprouechasse como desseauan. El obispo que
tambiê auia de proueer alas necessidades (que no me-
nores q otras eran) de su obispado: coligio el presente
auiso: por elqllos confessores se rigiessen/reduziêdo lo
a doze reglas. Y porq enla primera y qnta bizo mêciõ de
ser los cõfessores obligados antes q absfuelua/ constre-
ñir alos penitêtes: q den cauciõ ydonea y juridica: y al
gunos religiosos lo tuuierõ por aspero pareciendo les
no ser caso delos dl derecho: porde para dar razõ desta
obligaciõ: hizo vna declaracion q nõbro addiciõ delas
dichas pmera yqnta reglas. Enla ql prueua cuidêtemê
te: auer casos: enlosqles los cõfessores son obligados d
precepto natural y diuino: a cõstreñir a los q cõfiessan:
q hagã la dicha cauciõ antes qlos absfuelua. Estas reglas y addiciõ: vierõ y examinarõ/aprouarõ y firmarõ
quatro maestros y dos presentados q tãbien son ya ma
estros en theologia/y son estos. El maestro Belindo
theologo antiguo: el maestro Mirãda: el maestro Cano: el maestro Mancio: el maestro Soto mayor: el maestro fray Francisco de sant Pablo.

FIG. 3 "Argumento del presente tractado" (The reason for the present tract) reads the first page of the first printed version of Bartolomé de Las Casas's 1552 *Confesionario*. Photograph courtesy of Biblioteca Nacional de Chile, Santiago.

guide themselves in the forum of conscience so that they might not harm themselves and that the penitents might benefit as they desired. The bishop, who also must have foreseen (not less than others) the needs of his bishopric, compiled the present advice by which the confessors might govern themselves, reducing it [the advice] to twelve rules.

[2] And [this is] because in the first and the fifth [rules] mention was made of the confessors being obliged before they might give absolution to compel penitents to give a suitable and juridical pledge [to make restitution]. Some religious hold this to be harsh, because

[it] seems to them there is no case for them in law. [T]herefore, in order to explain this obligation, [the bishop] made a declaration, which he called an *Adición to the said first and fifth rules,* in which he proves manifestly that there are cases in which the confessors are obliged by natural and divine precept [and canon law] to compel those who confess to make the said pledge before they are absolved.²

[3] The *Doce reglas* rules and the *Adición* were seen, examined, approved, and signed by four masters and two *presentados* (theologians), who are also now masters in theology, and they are these: Master [Domingo] Galindo [O.P., d. 1580], senior theologian; Master [Bartolomé de Carranza y] Miranda [O.P., d. 1576]; Master [Melchor] Cano [d. 1560]; Master Mancio [de Corpus Christi]; Master [Peter de] Sotomayor [d. 1563]; and the master friar Francisco de San Pablo.

Prologue

[4] The confessors who might hear the confessions of penitents in the Indies or those of other individuals in different places in the Indies who might have been conquistadors in those places or who might have had or have Indians from repartimiento or who might have acquired part of their monies with Indians or from Indians should observe and govern themselves by the following twelve rules.³

---

2. This paragraph introduces the *Adición de la primera y quinta reglas,* the appendix to the original *Doce reglas* presented in the second half of the published *Avisos y reglas.*

3. The colonial system of repartimiento (or *mita* in Peru and *cuatequil* in New Spain) consisted of the apportionment or allotment of indigenous people as laborers. Beginning in the early colonial period, the indigenous peoples quickly became the source of forced labor. This administrative act was usually done by the viceroy or the audiencia in response to Spaniards' request for laborers, for example, in mines, on plantations or ranches, or in seasonal agricultural work to produce essential foods and goods. Frequently, this system mandated indigenous labor three and four times annually for a work period of two weeks. After the New Laws in 1542, the repartimiento became a paid labor force, especially in mines, factories, and public works, and included the mandatory purchase of goods by the indigenous workers. Initially, the repartimiento allotted indigenous laborers, whereas the encomienda referred to the governance and actual operation of that labor force. Both systems resulted in what Las Casas condemned as the "hardest, harshest, and most heinous bondage" of the native inhabitants of the Americas. Las Casas, *Brevísima relación,* in *Obras completas,* 10:35.

I.

[5] The first rule pertaining to this present matter concerns three classes of persons who come to confess themselves: [the first] are conquistadors; [the second are] settlers having Indians from apportionment (they are also called *comenderos*)[4] or having encomiendas of Indians; the third is merchants, not all of them, but those who carried arms and merchandize to those who were conquering and making war on the Indians; thus [they too] engaged in bellicose actions. If [the penitent] might be a conquistador and, as such, might want to confess at death's door; before they [confessor and penitent] begin the confession, a public scribe, or [notary], of the king must be called, and [the confessor] must make the [penitent] declare, order, and concede by public act the following things:

[6] First, [the penitent] must assert and say that he, as a faithful Christian, desires to leave this life without offense to God and to unburden his conscience, in order to appear before the divine judge in a secure state. [Also], he chooses whatever confessor, secular priest, or religious of some Order and gives him complete power (insofar as he [the penitent] is able and is obliged by divine and human law to unburden his conscience) in all that he [the confessor] might consider suitable for his [the penitent's] salvation. And if it might seem to the said confessor that it is necessary to make restitution with [the penitent's] entire hacienda,[5] in the way that might seem to him [the confessor] that it ought to be restored, without leaving anything for his heirs, he can freely do this, just as this same patient or penitent would have been able and ought to have done freely during his life for the security of his soul.[6] And in this case, [the penitent] subjects

4. *Comenderos*, or encomenderos, received the benefice, an encomienda, on condition of swearing allegiance to the king of Spain.

5. A precise definition of *hacienda* is impossible, since the term may refer to public and private property located within, near, or at a distance from Spanish or indigenous villages, including mines, ranches, *estancias* (private land holdings), sugar plantations, hereditary encomiendas, or large estates. This property might have had buildings as well as on-site managers or owners. Extraction industries and agricultural enterprises (such as livestock raising) might have taken place on this land. Las Casas seems to define haciendas in a variety of ways, although predominantly as landholdings, their buildings, and income-generating enterprises, which had access to the indigenous peoples as forced laborers—all of which constituted the owner's wealth or fortune.

6. Las Casas refers to the penitent in medical terms, which he does again later in the *Adición*.

the said entire hacienda to [the confessor's] judgment and opinion, without any condition nor limitation.

[7] Second, the scribe [one taking the testimony] declares and affirms that [the penitent] was found in such and such conquests or wars against Indians in these Indies and that he did or helped to carry out robberies, violence, injuries, deaths, and capture of Indians and destructions of many villages and places that in them and throughout them they did.

[8] Third, the scribe declares and affirms that [the penitent] did not bring any hacienda from Castilla, but all that he has is from the Indians, or with Indians, although some things he might possess from agricultural profits. And he is to affirm that the sum of all he amassed from Indians and is owed to Indians—together with the harms that he did and helped to do after arriving in the Indies—is so great that another abundant hacienda in addition to his own would not be enough to make satisfaction to them. And, therefore, if he might wish and his ultimate desire is that the said confessor may satisfy and restore everything fully, at least insofar as [the penitent's] hacienda might suffice, he might see his soul fulfilled. And concerning this, [the penitent] intimately entrusts his conscience [to the confessor].

[9] Fourth, if [the penitent] might have had any Indians as slaves, by whatever way, title, or manner he might have had or those he might have, then immediately and at once he is to grant them irrevocable freedom, without any limitation or condition. Also, he is to ask them to pardon him for the injury he did to them in making them slaves, usurping their liberty, or in helping, or in being part of whatever might have made them so; or if he did not do it, for having purchased, possessed, and served himself with slaves in bad faith. Because this is certain, and the confessor must know it, there is no Spaniard in the Indies who may have acted in good faith, concerning four things. The first concerns the wars of conquest. The second concerns the fleets that were assembled from the Islands to Tierra Firme to transport assaulted and kidnapped Indians. The third concerns the enslaving and buying of Indians who had been sold as slaves. The fourth concerns the carrying and selling of arms and merchandise for the tyrant conquistadors, when they were actually engaged in the conquests, violence, and tyrannies. And [the confessor] shall mandate that the said Indians whom he had as slaves be paid what he [the penitent] owed them for each month or each year—all that the

discrete confessor might judge as recompense for [the Indians'] work and service and the injury done to them.

[10] Fifth, [the penitent] revokes any other will or codicil that he might have made, affirming that he wishes only this one alone may be valid and firm and that it be fulfilled as his final will. And, if it might also be necessary, he gives power to the said confessor to add a clause or clauses to [the penitent's will] in favor of the said restitution and satisfaction whatever [the confessor] might see as fitting for the health of [the penitent's] soul. [In this way], [the confessor] must clear up any doubts that might arise about this business and may order anything that might be better suited to unburden [the penitent's] conscience.

[11] Sixth, [the penitent] must make a solemn oath in accord with law and obligation [that] cover[s] all of his personal property and real estate [and] that he will keep and complete [the oath] and assent to what the said confessor might order and command him to do with all his goods, nothing excluded. And if it might happen that he escape that [terminal] illness, he will not revoke this testament in whole or in part in his lifetime nor at the time of his end and death; neither shall he make another declaration by another testament nor a codicil contrary to what was said. And as long as he might live, he will be [bound] by the rules that the said confessor might give to him [and] that will be put below about conquistadors who are not at death's door. And if something might happen or might be done contrary to what is said above, in whole or in part, [the penitent] gives power to the bishop, his prelate, and the ecclesiastical judiciary; and, if it might be necessary to effect this, to [call on] the secular judiciary, to assure that [the penitent] may be punished for perjury and might complete all that is said, omitting nothing. Of course, he is divested of all his goods and makes transfer [of them] and subjects them to ecclesiastical jurisdiction, so as to compel him to fulfill all that he agreed to, and he renounces whatever laws that may help him contest the above agreement.

II.

[12] Second rule: that after the aforesaid [public pledge] is made and signed, the confessor may hear the confession of the said penitent; this [pledge] may greatly move [the penitent] so that he may

have very great sorrow and repentance for his very grave sins, that are those he committed by doing or helping to do such great harms and evils to the Indians: unsettling, robbing, killing, and depriving them of their liberties, of their *señoríos*,[7] of their wives, of their children and of their other possessions; making many widows, many orphans, [and] defaming them as if they were beasts; and by the incredible cruelties against them [that the penitent] did and helped to do and especially the vileness and abomination that he caused to the name of Christ and to the holy faith. And about the damnation of the [indigenous] souls he killed before their time—taking from them the time and space for repentance and their conversion, [the Indians] today are burning in the flames of hell. Also [the Spaniards] having been the initiators and cause of the oppression and tyranny that then [these Indians] have suffered, still suffer and will suffer daily in the services [rendered to the Spaniards] and the daily vexations.

[13] He must do penance not only for what he did by his [own] hands but also for all the evils and harms that others did [or] with whom he collaborated, because every one of them is obliged *in solidum*.[8] The reason for this is because all those who went to conquer knew very well [why] they were going; and all of them carried that intention and, just as they carried it [the intention to conquer], they fulfilled and put it into effect. They never had the authority of the king to do the wrongs they did. And even if they might have had it, this would not have been a sufficient excuse for them, nor was there legitimate cause to wage those most unjust wars that displaced the Indians [but was driven] only by their great ambition and insatiable greed. And, therefore, each one (at least those [settlers] who attacked the Indians who were secure in their houses in order to sell them as slaves, and we suppose here that none of [the settlers] acted in good faith; but if by chance one of them acted in good faith, another judgment must be made regarding him; concerning this case, there is enough written).[9] Such a one is obliged to lament for all of those

7. *Señoríos* refers to the jurisdiction, dominion, territories, and estates belonging to indigenous lords.

8. Las Casas held that each Spaniard was liable for the whole "debt"—for all that was owed in restitution to the indigenous people.

9. While Las Casas seemed to make all-inclusive statements about *mala fe*, in this statement, he left room for exceptions. He did the same with respect to his statement about invincible ignorance.

they offended and to restore everything that all of them robbed and acquired so wickedly and the damages that they did; even though he might not have possessed or enjoyed [a single] *maravedí* out of one hundred thousand million [that was taken], he is obliged to restore the entire one hundred thousand million.[10]

III.

[14] Third rule: that the confessor, [having] seen an inventory of all the goods of the penitent, may know and might consider the places where he and his co-defendants or companions did harm and evil to the Indians. If the victims, or their heirs, might still be alive, [the confessor] orders him to pay what might seem fitting, making a public document of all he might order or command. If the said [victims and heirs] might not still be alive, he may make it [restitution] for the good of the same villages, if they might not have not been entirely destroyed; [then the penitent] may bring in Indians from other parts to set up residence for themselves in these villages and give them the wherewithal to live or on what [land] and how they may begin to live. Or [the penitent] could free Indians who are now enslaved [by other Spaniards], since the tyranny and lack of the fear of God and of eternal damnation does not move those holding Indians as slaves to free them.

[15] And if this might not take place, because there are no villages that may not already be destroyed nor [have] any means to reconstruct them, then the penitent may restore that hacienda in three ways: [1] That he dedicate, delegate, and spend himself making villages for Spaniards; if being many, [he] goes to borderlands of the region of the land or the province where the harms were done. [2] Or in the villages already built by Spaniards more closely neighboring the province or provinces that he helped to destroy, he may introduce or increase poor *vecinos* (Spanish landholding residents) in them and of the poor, the most virtuous of them, giving to them part of that hacienda, with which they may live or may be able to

---

10. A *maravedí* is the smallest value of old Spanish coinage; its worth fluctuated at different times.

begin to live as landholding residents.[11] [3] And if it might be that
such a hacienda or haciendas is for all [that is, held in common],
apply part [of the income] so that a pledge may be made in a way to
invest this income in Seville[12] for food and to help purchase books
and other necessities [to be used] while the three religious [mendi-
cant] Orders[13] are there [and] who, with the license of the king, might
go to preach and teach the Indians in these Indies. Also, the penitent
can spend a third to bring married laborers, few or many, according
to the hacienda or haciendas that should sustain them, in order that
they may populate these lands.

IV.

[16] Fourth rule: although the deceased may have a hundred
legitimate children,[14] there must neither be given nor applied to them
a maravedí, even if owed to them by law, nor may it come to them
by inheritance, nor may they have a part in that hacienda. [These
heirs] can be given, by way of alms, only what might seem suitable
to the confessor for their sustenance. Also [the confessor] is able to
give them [the wherewithal] so that they can become landholding
residents in neighboring villages, as is said above [in rule 3], and he
is able to prefer them to other strangers *ceteris paribus* (all things
being equal) and in no other way. The reason for the first part of this
rule is because none of these conquistadors has a single maravedí that

11. *Vecinos* were the earliest landholding Spanish residents in the Indies. However, definitions of *vecino* vary. In the fifteenth century, the term was used to refer
to people having a place and to point out that they were legitimate children of their
parents; later the term implied a family unit, then just a resident of a certain place, and
occasionally as a high-status person or nobility. The term also became used to desig-
nate a resident or neighbor. The best contemporary definition seems to be a "landholding Spanish resident."

12. *Comprar* is the Spanish verb used here, which can also mean to buy off or
bribe, to win over, or to secure allegiance of. Also note that Las Casas referred to
Seville—the commercial capital of the Spanish Empire.

13. The mendicant Orders were Dominican, Franciscan, and Augustinian.

14. The word *hijos* can be translated as either "children" or "sons"—"sons" is
seemingly the meaning here. Las Casas also seems to imply multiple heirs rather than
one heir, as would have been the common practice in Spain, where, according to the
custom of *mayorazgo*, the oldest male child received all the inheritance, especially any
family property.

may be his own; even if before each one of them might have had such high status and great wealth as that of the duke of Medinasidonia [sic],[15] it would not satisfy the restitution and satisfaction for what he is obligated. Therefore, since he does not have anything of his own, he does not have anything to leave his children or his heirs to inherit.

V.

[17] Fifth rule: if the penitent might not be in danger of death, but [while healthy] might want to confess himself, the confessor must to come an agreement before [beginning the sacrament] with the penitent and ask him if he wants to remove all doubt and to put his conscience in a secure state. And if [the penitent] might respond affirmatively with his whole heart, [the confessor] orders him to make a public document by which he obligates himself to agree with what the confessor might determine and order as fitting to his conscience concerning his entire hacienda, although all [wealth] may be expended [in order to make restitution]. And in order to have and assure firmly and completely as the confessor might order and command, [the penitent] pledges all his goods in the same way as was said in the first rule, giving power to the bishop of that diocese and to the ecclesiastical judiciary so that they may constrain or compel the penitent in the juridical ecclesiastical forum to all that was said above.

[18] This rule, along with the first, is confirmed clearly and formally in the same terms as in the chapter "Super eo. de raptoribus,"[16] where it is established by Pope Eugene III that confessors may not absolve kidnappers, as are all the said conquistadors of the Indies, unless first they might restore all that was stolen or might give "restituendi, seu emendandi firmam et plenam securitatem, et cétera" (by restoring, by correcting firmly and [with] full assurance, and so forth). And thus states the text and places there grave penalties on the confessor who might do the contrary. Also, this may be proven

15. At the time of Las Casas, the duke of Medina Sidonia held title to the oldest dukedom in the kingdom of Castile. Once the most prominent aristocrats of Andalusia, the *grandees* of this magnate family dated the beginning of their titles from the reign of King John II of Castile (1406–54) onward.

16. Las Casas directs the reader to the *Decretals of Gregory IX*, bk. 5, title 17, chs. 2–3. See also *Decretum of Gratian*, "De poenitentia," dist. 6, ch. 1.

from the chapter [titled] "Quanquam, de usuris" in book 6 [although it focuses on interest].[17]

VI.

[19] Sixth rule: the said juridical guarantee and assurance having been made, the confessor observes and examines whether the penitent is rich and if he has villages of Indians who may pay him tribute and what revenue he has. If this income is yielding (as they say) and certain, he distinguishes that revenue from tributes or what may be from agricultural profits. With such a penitent, he must do, order, and command the following: First, assess the ordinary cost of [the penitent's] eating, drinking, and clothing—his own and that of his wife and children—if there is any, only what is necessary and no

17. Las Casas included the text of this "chapter" as part of his footnote. "Statuimus, ut quicumque ex his, qui violenter surrexerint in rapinam, sive Ecclesiarum violationes, manifeste fuerit deprehensus: nisi prius ablata restituat, si potuerit, vel emendandi firmam et plenam securitatem fecerit, poenitentiae beneficium ei penitus denegetur. Si vero usque ad obitum in contumacia sua duraverit, et in extremis positus, remedium poenitenitae humiliter postulaverit, si emendationem, vel emendandi securitatem praestiterit, ei poenitentia et sepultura Ecclesiastica concedatur. Qui autem in sanitate, obstinata mente non poenituerit vel emendaverit, et in morte securatatem praestare nequiverit, solennitas poenitentiae parum prodesse videtur, sicut credimus; sed de peccato contrito viaticum non denegetur, ita tamen, ut nullus clericorum sepulturae illius intersit, nec ejus eleemosynam praesumat accipere. Quod si quis Presbyterorum vel Clericorum contra hoc in vita vel morte poenitentias dare, aut sepulturae interesse, vel eorum eleemosynas accipere attentaverit, seu hujusmodi rapiae participes inventi fuerit, ordinis sui dam num irreparabiliter patiantur, et Ecclesiastico beneficio carenat." (We decree that, in the case of one who is clearly guilty of defacing and pillaging a church, the benefit of the sacrament will surely be denied to him, unless he has already restored the stolen property or firmly attested his intention of making full restitution. If such a one should remain obstinate to the point of death but humbly petitions the remedy of penance, then as long as he shall have made restitution, or a pledge thereof, the church will agree to absolve and bury him. But for one who neither repents nor atones while he is in good health and is able to make no such pledge when he is already deceased, we believe that the external manifestation of penance will not help much; though he may receive the viaticum upon confessing his sins, no priest may grant him a Christian burial or receive his alms. And if any priest or cleric should give such persons absolution either in life or in death or preside at their burial or try to receive their alms, although they are known to have participated in such plundering, he shall irreparably lose his clerical status as well as his ecclesiastical privileges.) Las Casas cited the *Decretals of Gregory IX*, vol. 2, bk. 5, title 17, p. 247. Thomas Irish, O.P., assisted in translating the Latin into English.

more; given that this [amount] is divisible, he might moderate his entire household's [spending] and adjust the dowry of his daughters in keeping with the rank of a person of low status. And the same if he were of wealthy lineage, place him in a very modest status, because it is not licit to live pompously out of someone else's property and in high status by means of the sweat of fellow human beings who owe him nothing. And see to it that each year his needs are met out of his modest sustenance, but only his necessities, as is said, and no more. And point out to [the penitent] that [what he receives] must be put to good use and that all the rest that might be left over of his income [which] may not come from Indians nor from their tributes, but from another source that he may already have or from [new and legitimate] profits, [that these] be restored by the same confessor or another faithful hand [of another person] in the way stated in the third rule. And best of all will be by the hand of the bishop, to whom the penitent may give power to carry it out, all the more since this comes under the jurisdiction [of the prelate] by law.

[20] Second, if some of those aggrieved by the conquests, or their heirs, are still alive, [and] if they might have suffered need, which for the Indians is never apt to be without extreme degree, the confessor must see that the penitent is obliged [to make restitution] by suffering [hardship] even if [the poverty] may be severe and extreme, [to make up to those] he robbed and by his tyranny put in such anguish and plight. This restitution must be made from the hacienda that he has, that is, not (as was said) from the tributes of the Indians.

[21] Third, impose on [the penitent] and command that all the tributes that he took since he began to take them must be repaid by the means and for the reason that will be stated in the seventh rule that follows.

[22] Fourth, command and impose on [the penitent] that he may not take any more tribute from [the Indians] thenceforth, but rather he is to defend and favor them and help and do indoctrination [of the Indians] at his own expense as soon as he might be able, and, hopefully, he may comply with this.

[23] Fifth, although [the penitent] may be a gentleman and of noble blood, he does not have the freedom to marry off his daughters or his sons as nobles, but as poor persons who possess nothing of their own.

[24] Sixth, if the penitent is not rich and has no revenue of the stated kind, he is not obliged to make the restitution that is owed for the harms and thefts of the conquests, other than by having the intention of satisfying [the obligation to make restitution] as if he might have [the means to do so] and to lament this all the days of his life.

[25] Seventh, he is obliged only to satisfy the Indians and their villages [to make restitution] from whom he takes and has taken tributes and also for the other ways he has aggrieved them, as will be said presently in the seventh and eighth rules.

[26] Eighth, in the case that the aggrieved and their heirs are all dead, part of the satisfaction would order [the penitent] to commit himself to remain on the land all of his life. [He does] this out of the respect he must have for the confessor to give him something more than the necessary goods that might have been restored [to him].

VII.

[27] Seventh rule: penitents who might not have been conquistadors, but settlers, and who might have had or might have Indians by repartimiento, if they might be at death's door, the confessor commands them to make restitution to those same persons for everything of theirs that they might have taken as tributes and services, this is if [the Indians] or their heirs might be alive, or [make restitution] to the villages where they were [from] so that all the Indians from the village or villages may be part of such restitution. And this may be understood as what seemed [to the confessor] as properly taken, inasmuch as he did not require more than what [the Indians] were assessed [in taxes or tributes]. Although they might have been properly assessed [in the eyes of the Spaniards], they in fact never were [properly assessed] but [rather were levied] unjustly, excessively, and tyrannically.

[28] The reason for this rule is twofold: first, because all the things that have been done throughout the Indies with the entrance of the Spaniards into each province as [well as] in the subjection and servitude in which they might have put these people, [along] with all the means and ends and all the rest that they have done to them and near

them, have been contrary to all natural law and the law of nations and also against divine law, and, therefore, is entirely unjust, iniquitous, tyrannical, and deserving of all eternal fire, and, consequently, null, invalid, and without any value and weight of law. And since all may be null and void by law, thus they were not able to take justly from the Indians one single maravedí of tribute, and as such [the Spaniards] are obliged to make restitution for all of it, for many and juridical reasons that there are, [but] that we are not offering here for the sake of brevity. Whoever is studious will be able to discover [these reasons for restitution] if he entrusts himself greatly to God, and [they] dig down deep until they find the foundations. Second, [the reason for this seventh rule] is because they have not fulfilled the final cause or the task that was put to them in the *cédulas* about such encomiendas, which was and is to preach to and to teach these people [the Christian faith], to which they [the encomenderos] were obliged, and they never accomplished it, not even in their dreams, nor did they provide that it be done; [on the contrary], they have hindered this [task] as if they were infidels. Concerning what they carried away besides the tributes, there is no need to consider nor doubt it, since it is certain that they robbed and possessed it by evil conduct. And regarding this restitution, there is no room for alms to children and to the widowed wife, since we suppose that the dispossessed and aggrieved owners or their heirs are still living. It is against justice to provide for some by means of the hacienda or the goods of others; it is to commit larceny.

VIII.

[29] Eighth rule: if the penitent encomendero to be confessed is not at death's door, but healthy, and if this one might be poor and may not have more than what the Indians give to him in tribute, [and] meanwhile if the condition of the Indians is as downtrodden as it is today, [such] that the Indians may be greatly or minimally taxed, the confessor can evaluate the condition and expenses of such a penitent in the same way as described in the sixth rule. [The confessor] orders [for restitution] that [the penitent] may not take only that amount and places [on the penitent] some other rules that might seem suitable to [the confessor] concerning this matter:

[the penitent] might be able to work [supporting the] teaching and indoctrinating by [members of the mendicant] religious [Orders], and he personally, as may be in accord with his ability, may teach and defend and provide for them and help and gain favor for them before magistrates and other persons, and, finally, may he aid and assist them with their needs.

[30] Likewise, may he be ready to receive what the king might order, and in no manner may [the penitent] entreat nor [in] any other manner, direct or indirect, resist [any] law or provision or mandate that the king might provide in this case before inducing others to obey and to carry it [what the king orders] out.[18] [This is] because this [entreating and resisting] must not be done or cannot be done without great offence to God, as [this type of behavior] would be to resist the welfare, tranquility, and preservation and liberty of his Indian neighbors, which is manifestly against the divine precept that commands us to love our neighbor. And what we would not wish for ourselves, we may not wish for other humans, since they owe us nothing. This support is given justly [to the inhabitant] so that [the inhabitant] may populate the land and may accompany the [spread of the] Christian religion. And if there might have been order in the Indies and the Spaniards might not have caused havoc, death, and harm to the Indians, justly the Indians might have been able to help them to be sustained on the land, for only the said end of sustaining the faith and their welfare would have resulted for the Indians from the presence of Spanish Christians.

[31] And if from such penitent they might ask the fourth part of the tributes, as ordered by the gathering of the bishops, held [in] the year 1546, now passed, [they shall] pay it from the tributes according to what might have been assessed. Concerning the tributes that he has taken since that time, he is obliged to make restitution; he may work for himself or for the religious so that the Indians may voluntarily and graciously, without fear, fraud, or deception, remit [the tribute] to them and pardon [the Spaniard] and [thus] exercise charity; or [the Spaniard might] give alms for it, and he must lament his blindness for the rest of his life. And this method and remedy ought

18. Seemingly, Las Casas might be saying this in part to offset any criticism he might receive concerning his loyalty to the king. He had faced accusations of treason before, so he knew how to avoid them as well as how to respond to detractors.

to be used by those who have great obligation to make restitution and do not have [resources] in these Indies.

[32] All that is said in these seventh and eighth rules concerning encomenderos must also be understood as applying to Spanish miners and ranchers, known in New Spain as *calpisques*.[19] They ought to be judged and constrained to repentance and restitution with more rigor, since they have been the most inhuman, cruel, and soulless, and the executioners and ministers of all perdition for the Indians who have perished and are perishing in the mines and in other daily works.

IX.

[33] Ninth rule: concerning the Indians who are possessed as slaves in whatever way they may be made [slaves] or by whatever title they are held, possessed, purchased, or obtained through inheritance or also purchased from Indians or received as tribute from villages of Indians, the confessor, without any doubt or scruple or delay, orders the penitent then at once to set them free by a public act before a notary and that he pay them all they were owed for each year and month that their services and labors merited, and this is to be done before [the confessor and penitent] may enter into confession. And in the same way [the penitent] asks pardon of them for the injury he did [to] them, as was said in the first rule. Because, [and] hold this as [is] very certain and verifiable by one who knows it well, that in all the Indies, since they were discovered until today, there has not been nor is there one nor any Indian [who] may have been justly enslaved. And the same judgement is [made] concerning those who were purchased from Indians, since scarcely will be found [an enslaved Indian] who ought to be considered truly a slave according to law. And if someone might be considered truly a slave or taken in wars that the Indians might have had among themselves or by their just laws, then what I am saying is not applicable concerning such a one.

[34] Concerning Indians whom Spaniards had as slaves, and [about those who] had been sold, the penitent is obliged to go back and

---

19. The term *calpisques* refers to those in charge when the owner of the haciendas or mines was absent.

purchase them for whatever price he may redeem them, even though he might have sold them for two [maravedís] and might not be able to ransom them but for a thousand [maravedís]. And if he does not have the means to buy them, Richard [de Mediavilla] says, in the 4°, di. 15 art. 15, q. 4, *ad* 2, *partis* 2, that [the penitent] is obliged to make himself a slave in order to free the one he unjustly sold as a slave.[20] This point we introduce here so that the gravity of the sin and the obligation for restitution may be known. And he ought to exercise great diligence in order to find out where is the one sold in order to liberate him. And if [the former slaves] might be dead, he may pay [the sum] for which he sold them and [an additional sum] for the service they provided him. And may he lament all the days of his life for the great sin and harm he did to his neighbors. This restitution for this may be given for the soul of the one or of those he sold, if they were Christians, or for the aforesaid works.

X.

[35] Tenth rule: if the penitent might be married, man or woman, [and] if the Indians they have as slaves are held jointly, as if they both might have acquired [them] during the marriage, the confessor must order and compel the penitent, if he is the husband, to draw lots so that he might determine and know his half [of the slaves] in order that they may be set free by the said means; in the same way, the confessor orders him to induce the wife so that she might to do the same with her part. But if the woman might be the one

20. This textual reference is regarding thirteenth-century Franciscan theologian Richard de Mediavilla (Richard of Middleton). *Super quarto sententiarum*. The theme is treated in 15 art. 5, qto., 100v–101v, and its directive is expressed in the following terms: "Dicendum quod damnificans alium iniuste in sua libertate, scilicet, iniuste procurando ipsum redigi in servitute: tenetur se facere servum pro eo, si non potest aliter restituere libertati, nisi forte talis esset conditio personae quae damnum intulit quod bonum notabiliter redundaret in praedictum boni communis; in quo casu non tenetur se facere servum, sed tenetur ad omne aliud interesse ad arbitrium bonorum." (It must be said of the one who unjustly ruins another person by selling them into slavery, that they are obliged to make themselves a slave in exchange for that person, unless they may otherwise restore the person to liberty. But if the condition of the victim is such that the aforementioned common good is notably increased, then they are not obliged to make themselves slaves, but must be of service in every other way ["ad omne aliud interesse"], according to the judgment of good people who are involved.)

confessing, and if the husband might be alive, [the confessor] cannot constrain her to free her half since, according to law, the husband has the administration of the hacienda, even if during the course of the marriage everything may belong to the woman. However, when later her husband is dying, she must be disposed to free those [slaves] who are his part and to pay them [the Indians] for their work and service; or if she might die first, that the same [must] be done by her last will and testament. Meanwhile, if she might see that it will be beneficial, she may induce her husband so that they might [free their Indians] together while they are both alive, and also, insofar as she should be able, she is always to regard and treat the Indians as free, which they were. In the same way, the confessor must have [an agreement] with the married couple about the tributes of Indians from repartimiento, if they were acquired and possessed jointly and also if they are totally hers. But if they are all his, it must be known whether he is in charge, so that the confessor might compel him to do and to complete what is contained in the aforementioned rules.

XI.

[36] Eleventh rule: the merchants who bring in arms like arquebus, gunpowder, crossbows, lances, and swords, and worst of all, horses, while the Spaniards are actually conquering and tyrannizing the Indians (as they are presently doing today in Peru and always have done in New Spain and Guatemala, Santa Marta, Venezuela, and in the other places), they have sinned mortally and are obligated to make restitution for all the evils, harms, and tyrannies they committed against all those they robbed, tyrannized, killed, and destroyed.

[37] The reason for this rule is because they were participants and with others caused those evils, thefts, and harms that were carried out with the help of the said arms; they did all those things. And they were not unaware, in small or large ways, [that] those wars and conquests were unjust. Or at least they should have doubted or were obligated to doubt the justice of them, and this is enough to place them in bad faith and that they may be culpable for all of it. In the same way, [for] the monies that they might have earned from the merchandise that they might have sold to [conquistadors], even if [the merchants] might not have carried arms, they are obligated to

pay restitution. Because those *predones* [thieves] and tyrants [con-quistadors] did not possess a thing that was not robbed, they paid [the merchants] with gold and silver that was robbed and [belonged] to another. And they [the merchants] remained impotent to make restitution at least for such merchandise such as wine, superfluous clothing, and gift items. All this we say supposing that [the mer-chants] did not have good faith, since if someone might be found of good faith, he may be directed by the confessor with the general rules that the doctors give, and the *Summas* are filled with them.

XII.

[38] Twelfth rule: this concerns two things that the confessor must dispose the penitent to hold by firm purpose in the future: First, that he may never again conquer or make war against Indians. This is because, throughout these many seasons and years, never will there be a just reason for the Spanish conquest against the Indians in these Indies of the Ocean Sea. Second, he may not go to Peru while tyrants there might be in rebellion against the king, for even though they may [claim] to obey to him, while at the same time they are destroy-ing and ravaging those peoples and being a disgraceful [example] of our holy faith to them.

[39] "Hec ora sunt durus sermo, et quis poterit eum audire? Qui voluerit ingredi arctam et laboriosam viam, quae ducit ad vitam."[21]

Appendix to the First and the Fifth Rules

[40] Because some will regard as harsh what is said in the first and fifth rules, namely for the confessor to order the penitent that he might make an obligation or a public document, and so on, [and] since the confessors may not have the duty to go and to search out the laws and reasons the doctors give for it, there must be placed here some things [rules] that are pertinent. What is worth noting are the

---

21. Las Casas cites Jn 6:11, which in the New American Bible (NAB) corresponds to Jn 6:60ab: "This saying is hard; who can accept it?" Las Casas also cites Mt 7:13: "Enter through the narrow gate; for the gate is wide and the road broad that leads to destruction, and those who enter through it are many." (Latin translation: The one who will wish to enter the narrow and difficult way that leads to life.)

two ways that the confessor might obligate the penitent to make the pledge or to guarantee restitution and satisfaction to others: the first, by obligation that he might have [to do] it; the second, because to him it might not seem to be an obligation. Regarding the first, he can be obligated in two ways: first, by canon law, which might constrain him by means of penalties; the second, by natural and divine law. And according to this, one is able to ask for the said pledge from the penitent in three ways.

[41] Concerning the first, in two cases the confessor is obliged by canon law under grave penalties to ask for the said pledge before confession or at least before he might absolve the penitent. The first [case refers] to those who were public kidnappers or thieves or who might have burned or transgressed churches, as appears in the chapter "Super eo, de raptoribus," in the *Decretals*, where there the text explains that if such kidnappers, arsonists, or transgressors of churches might be made known, and they might not have first restored what they have robbed, or if they might have done this and have not given firm and full assurance to make restitution, not just for what they have robbed but also for the harms done by such robberies, as the doctors note there, the Sacrament of Penance may be totally denied them; that is, their confessions may not be heard or at least they may not be absolved or receive the rest that pertains to the said sacrament. And if they might persist throughout their lives in contempt and hardness, and at death's door with humility and contriteness of heart they might ask for the remedy of the Sacrament of Penance, if they might make restitution or might give the said assurance of restitution, in this case, the pope commands that [the Sacrament of] Penance may be granted to them, which means that their confession may be heard and they may be absolved [and might receive] the rest that affects and concerns the said sacrament. But if in life [they persist] with an obstinate heart or might not have done penance or restituted and satisfied for the robberies and harms they did, at death's door they might not be able to make restitution or satisfaction; if they might have contrition in their hearts, the confessor can absolve them and give them the holy sacrament of the Eucharist, but no cleric may dare to be found at their burial or receive any alms from them, given that laypeople may bury them in the cemetery in accordance with what the doctors say. And this is resolved and commanded there because of the terror and destruction of such a great crime.

[42] The text further says, concerning these types of individuals who might not want to make restitution or to give full and firm assurance to make restitution and satisfaction as is said, if some priest or cleric might be so bold as to hear their confessions, either in life or at death, and to absolve them, or they might have attended their funeral and interment or might have received some alms from them or might have participated in the said robberies, they [these confessors] must be stripped irretrievably of their Orders [faculties] and deprived of any ecclesiastical benefits they might have.

[43] The second case, in which the confessor is obliged by [canon] law to ask for the suitable pledge before he may hear the confession of a penitent and may absolve [him], is when the penitent is a public moneylender, as appears in the chapter "Quanquam, de usuris," in book 6.[22] And since [this example] does not aid our proposition, there is no need to speak more about it.

[44] There are other cases in [canon] law concerning the excommunicated, in which first they must give a pledge [to make restitution] so that they may be absolved, but since the greater part of this pertains to the juridical ecclesiastical forum, [and] also does not have anything to with our case, it is not necessary to spend time on it. The opinion appears in the chapter "Ex parte, de verborum significationibus."[23] And these cases are treated at length in the *Summa confessorum*, bk. 3, title 34, q. 136.[24]

[45] The second kind of obligation, according to which the confessor may ask or ought to ask for a pledge [of restitution] from the penitent, is from natural and divine law.[25] For understanding what is to be considered from divine and natural law, the confessor is obligated to provide the penitent in counsel and advice and mandate all that is suitable for the good and security of his conscience, thus about the avoidance of evil and the apprehension and pursuit of the good, as reasonably [the confessor] would and should want to do for the health of the suffering soul; about that [see] Matthew 7: "Omnia

22. Las Casas treats a theme that appears in *Decretals of Gregory IX*, bk. 3, title 16, p. 248, note 3.

23. *Decretals of Gregory IX*, bk. 5, title 40, chs. 23, 30, and 31. [ABP]

24. Bartolomé is referring to the *Summa confessorum* of Raymond of Peñafort. [ABP]

25. In paragraphs 41 to 44, Las Casas deals with the obligation from canon law; from paragraphs 45 to 50, he deals with natural and divine law.

quaecumque vultis ut faciant vobis homines, et vos facite illis."[26] And, on the contrary, as [stated] in Tobit 4: "What we do not want for ourselves . . ."[27] And Matthew 22 [says], "Diliges proximum tuum sicut te ipsum."[28]

[46] Likewise, the confessor is a spiritual judge, placed by God in his universal church for the usefulness and benefit of souls, especially for that which is placed in his hands in the rite of confession, which [the confessor] is obligated by natural and divine law to judge justly, exercising justice, that is, to faithfully carry out office and to be the faithful and prudent servant; according to that, [see] Matthew, chapter 24: "Quis putas est fidelis servus et prudens quem constituit dominus super familiam suam, ut det illis in tempore tritici,s., in confessione, mensuram, quam secundum iusticiam et prudentiam determinare debet."[29] And the apostle in 1 Corinthians 4 says, "Sic nos existimet homo, ut ministros Christi et dispensatores ministeriorum dei. Hic iam queritur inter dispensatores, ut fidelis quis inveniatur."[30] [See] also 1 Peter 4: "Unusquisque sicut accepit gratiam in alterutrurm illa in administrantes, sicut boni dispensatores," et cetera.[31]

[47] As such, since God placed the confessor in that office, it is the time and the reason or the opportunity to bring up the [divine] precept [of love of neighbor] for the exercise of the work of charity and almsgiving, which counsel [the confessor] ought to give to the penitent, when [the confessor] is in the act of confession and as such is spiritual judge (as appears in *De peni.*, distin. 6, cap. 1).[32]

26. Mt 7:12a: "Do to others whatever you would have them do to you. This is the law and the prophets."

27. Seemingly, Las Casas refers to Tob 4:15a: "Do to no one what you yourself hate."

28. Mt 22:39: "You shall love your neighbor as yourself."

29. Mt 24:45: "Who then is the faithful and prudent servant, whom the master has put in charge of his household to distribute to them their food at the proper time?"

30. Cor 4:1–2: "Thus should one regard us: as servants of Christ and stewards of the mysteries of God. Now it is of course required of stewards that they be found trustworthy."

31. 1 Pt 4:10: "As each one has received a gift, use it to serve one another as good stewards of God's varied grace."

32. Las Casas does not specify from what tract he extracts this citation of *De poenitentia* to which he alludes. There were many additions of the *Summae*, as well as many glosses, to help confessors in cases of conscience. See the *Summa confessorum* of Raymond of Peñafort and the *Margarita confessorum*, published by Baltanás Domingo, O.P., of San Pablo in Seville in 1526, fols. 93–96. Also consult the *Decretals domini* of Pope Gregory IX *diligentia tertio emendata* (the emended third devotion),

The confessor is obligated to order what is suitable to [the penitent's] spiritual health and to do justice to those [that the penitent] might have wronged or dispossessed, commanding him to carry out the required restitution and satisfaction in a manner that may be effective. The sentence that the confessor might give for such restitution and satisfaction may not be frustrated, yet rather may it be executed and done in due course. [Yet] the prudent confessor [may] see that in some case it is beneficial to the soul of the penitent to leave with the effect of the sin of injustice—that of retaining another's [property] against the owner's will. [However], in order to be certain that such restitution and satisfaction may be done for the aggrieved and the deprived, before confession [the penitent] must make a suitable and sufficient pledge to show that he is obligated by natural and divine law. Because, in this way, he would accept what the confessor might have done [according to divine and natural law] [and] may confess to the confessor about the one he might have aggrieved and deprived, and [thus] doing justice may be effective and would not frustrate what is from natural and divine law.

[48] Then there are cases from natural and divine law—not expressed in [canon or civil positive] law—in which the confessor will be obligated to demand and constrain the [penitent] so that he may give a suitable and sufficient pledge, even before confession. At present, there are three cases that might occur in which, according to the consensus of the doctors, the confessor seemingly will be obligated by natural and divine law to ask for the said pledge and to constrain the penitent, at least before he may absolve him, and in other similar examples, expressly being public debts, those in which the deserving and dispossessed are not able to obtain justice. The first [case] is when the quantity and size [of the debt], as is fitting to know, concerns a great sum of money and burdens for such restitution, and this because of the great difficulty there may be in making such restitutions and almost an impossibility, since, as we see, barely of ten thousand [owed], he [hardly repays] one [for the ten thousand owed]. The second [case is] when the penitent has gone to confession many times, and the confessors have ordered him to make restitution

---

especially book 5, which is an addition with numerous glosses. Also consult *Decretals domini of Pope Gregory IX*, especially book 5, which is an addition with numerous glosses.

and he has not done it, because it is presumed that he will make [the restitution] in the future, and this is called vehement presumption (s. *digna*), for which the said pledge may be asked. The third [case is] where the confessor might observe that because of habits and weak devotion or little fear of God that he senses in the penitent, [the confessor] will be able to presume vehemently that after leaving confession [the penitent] would do little to carry out the said restitution. These examples may be proven convincingly from the argument in the chapter "De presumptione," where there it is ordered to take a sure pledge. [This is so] that [the penitent] would complete the penalty or penance that might have been given to him in the [secular] juridical forum, the one whom was presumed would not complete it [otherwise]. [This] corresponds to 1. *Si fidei iussor*, § fi., ff. *qui satis dare cogum.*, and the gloss, in the 1. penultimate, ff. *de peti., heredi.*[33]

[49] And there must be no misunderstanding about what we are saying here, that in the forum of penance, the confessor must ask for a pledge that [the penitent] will do the penance that might be imposed on him, at least against his will, as Panormitano says in chapter "Literas"; rather [the confessor] can ask him for the said pledge that will restore what might have been illegally obtained from the rightful owner.[34] And in this, one can and ought to do in the three aforementioned cases and similar ones.

[50] We add the fourth [case], no less just and necessary than the others mentioned above, when the confessor might notice that in some matters there are diverse opinions—most of them not being [from] those who have much expertise and authority—[rather than from one who] has knowledge or probable opinion and sufficient reasons, [acquired] by great study, expertise, or experience of such a matter; [this is] distinguishable among those who have administration of justice, ecclesiastical as well as secular, [and] who are known to claim some interest or have some passion or liking and, with this, what he pursues is in favor of the public good and of those who are little able and [also] in order to avoid sins or injustices. And also if

33. See *Decretals of Gregory IX*, title 23. [BLC, *Avisos*]
34. See Panormitano, *Commentari*, bk. 2, title 23, ch. 14; and his *Super tertio decretaluim*, beginning with folio 110. Bartolomé also cites the chapter "Literas" from the *De praesumptionibus* of Gregory IX, *Liber Extra*, bk. 2, title, 23, ch. 14. The citation is found after *Digesta*, bk. 2, title 8, ch. 7; and in the *Glossa ordinaria* from the *Codex*, titled *De petitione hereditatis* (c. 3.31.12). [ABP]

[the remedy] is joined to the said permission or dissimulation of secular justice, or [if] by blindness [they] do not sense the gravity of the
damage to consciences, or because it seems to them that the temporal
good or utility of the republic would suffer detriment; therefore,
in [this] kind of judgement and said temporal justice, the aggrieved
and deprived do not have any remedy. Since all the aforementioned
conditions that might come together in this matter deal with the
harms and offenses and tyrannies committed against the Indians, the
confessor, without any doubt or trepidation, must order the penitent
to give the said suitable and sufficient pledge, even before they enter
into confession, which it seems without any doubt to us, that the said
confessor is obliged to do this from natural and divine law for the
aforementioned reasons.

[51] And in order to corroborate all the aforementioned, it is
worth advising that since the confessor, as was said, is the spiritual
judge and consequently also a public and official person of the universal church in all things that might concern souls and their spiritual office, as appears in the chapter "Ius publicum," dist. I, in the
decree where it is said, "Ius publicum est in sacris et sacerdotibus
et magistratibus,"[35] and the same is said in the ff. "de iusti. et iu.,"
in the first law;[36] and, therefore, the said confessor is able to receive
[an] obligation and to obligate the penitent to another, asking him
[the penitent] to obligate himself to pay the other that quantity or
large sum that it seems that he [the penitent] owes, which in law
is called stipulation. By this, the penitent remains obligated as if
he had made the obligation before a mayor or a public notary or
before a bishop. Therefore, whatever that the penitent confesses
in sacramental confession [about what] he owes or is responsible
for something to another, and if [the confessor] might not want to
absolve him if he does not promise to him [the confessor] or make
an obligation to pay or to restore to [the one due] restitution within
a specified time, although he may not make [the pledge] before a
notary, from that promise, although it may be a simple promise,

35. *Decretum of Gratian, Treatise on Laws*, dist. 1, c. 11; *Digesta of Justinian*,
1.1.1. [ABP]
36. The theme of the binding character of the words of the priest in the internal
forum of sacramental confession is frequent among the moralists and canonists, as well
as clear in pontifical decrees. The imprecise citation of Las Casas does not facilitate
locating the manual from which this proceeds.

or from that obligation, belongs action and law in such a way that the [deserving] party or creditor or deprived can appeal to the judiciary, and [the penitent] will be ordered to pay as if the obligation might have been made (as I said) before a public notary. And this Bártolo [de Sassoferrato (d. 1357)] and Alexandre [Tartagnus (d. 1477)] and Jasón [de Mayno (d. 1519)] say [as much] in the 1.1a, & *huius studi; ad finem,* ff. *de iusti. et iu.,* and the *Spec.,* in the title *de instrumen. edi., in & nunc vero aliqua. in versi. item pone quod quidam,* and, best of all, [as says] Innocencio in the final chapter "De sepulturis." It can [also] be proven from the chapter "Quanquam, de usuris," book 6;[37] [and] at length by Antonio de Butrio in the preface of the *Decretals,* [in the] penultimate column, where he gathers from among other [sources, such as from] Oldrado [da Ponte] in his thirtieth admonition, where, [along] with many notable things, he says in the said chapter "Quanquam" that the confessor may receive a pledge, which is not meant only in the case of usury but, also generally, in all the pertinent cases associated with the priest's office.[38]

[52] And, finally, the common opinion of legists and canonists is that the confessor can stipulate and oblige one [party] to pay another, and this [obligation] pertains to that creditor, and to all to whom it belongs by action and law this can be asked (as is said). And [in support of this] the doctors gather [arguments] in the said chapter "Quanquam,"[39] and they [also] bring 1. *non quasi,* ff. *rem pupilli fal. fo.* into the argument.[40] And they say more, that although the confessor may not have demanded an expressed pledge, it is seen to be given tacitly by the penitent the hour that he does his penance and asks for absolution from the confessor, if he absolves him. The reason for this is because he did not have any other way to make true repentance nor to save himself if [the confessor] had not ordered [him] to make restitution; then he tacitly obliged himself by receiving the benefit of absolution. For this [reason] the heirs can be asked and

37. The original *Confesionario* text states that Las Casas's reference makes us think of the commentaries of Bártolo de Sassoferrato on the *Codex* and on the *Digesta.*
38. Again, Las Casas provided his reader with the following detailed information. Oldrado da Ponte da Lodi, *Aurea ac pene diuina consilia iurium fontis vberrimis Bo. Oldradi de Ponte de Luade,* that is to say, the known *Consilia et quaestiones,* fols. 10, 19.
39. *Liber sextus decretalium* of Boniface VIII, "De usuris," in *Decretals of Gregory IX,* bk. 5, title 5, ch. 2. [ABP]
40. *Digesta of Justinian,* 46.6.4. [ABP]

constrained to make [the restitution] if the penitent might die and, if he is alive, to constrain him so that he may pay it in the exterior forum.

[53] Abbot Panormitano treats this [issue] in the final chapter, "De sepulturis," in the antepenultimate column.[41] Since the confessor may be judge and public person placed by God [as an] official of the universal church between the penitent and the deprived or aggrieved, [who] against justice lack what is his, [and] in order to compensate in the forum of penance for the defects, and what he [the confessor] is unable to free through the exterior judiciary forum, which he may obligate the penitent and acquire by right and action [in favor of] the creditor by asking him [the penitent] [during confession for] a pledge so that the end of confession is achieved, which is that the penitent may depart from sin and that the dispossessed may receive justice. It follows that in the aforesaid cases, the confessor is obliged to constrain the penitent by refusing him absolution, to which the said pledge may be sworn as a necessary thing, in order that restitution may be effected. Thus the conscience of the penitent will be assured, the aggrieved and the deprived will attain justice, and the confessor will fulfill his duty as a good public judge, even if exercised at great personal risk.

[54] And because, according to what we see, secular justices devote themselves little to what the sacred canons have ordered, which according to them and the law of God belong to the office of the priests, as a result, [they] will not want to constrain those such obliged by the stipulation of the confessor or [even] believe what he might say to him; therefore, it is necessary that if the debt or burden is secret and the creditor ignores it, and there is no danger that it may be known, the said confessor may constrain the penitent before giving him the benefit of absolution, in one of two [ways]:

[55] [First], he may make or give the said pledge signed by his own hand and oblige himself by it, with suitable witnesses, to pay and to restitute within a certain time period for what he is indebted. In order to fulfill [this pledge], he gives power to the ecclesiastical judiciary and subjects himself to it; because they may be able

---

41. Panormitano, "De sepulturis," vol. 3, fol. 133ff, note 10. In this treatise he establishes the principle, *Sepeliri non debet in sacro moriens in peccato mortali.* [BLC, *Avisos*]

to constrain him or his heirs to such restitution, [they may] give
license to that confessor who having discovered in confession from
him that debt or burden [owed]; he may give part of [the case] to the
prelate and ecclesiastical judiciary so that [the penitent] may give
pledges worth the owed amount. This is the best and most sure [way
to proceed] when the debt might be secret, and the creditor ignores
it. And, in this case, in order to exercise his duty most honestly, the
confessor must make the penitent aware of how he receives those
pledges for such end and such and such cause. However, if the debt is
manifest and there is no remedy from the secular judiciary, according
to civil law, one cannot be constrained to pay or to make the restitution that is owed. There are many cases in human laws in which no
one is obliged because, as was said above, of the blindness or avarice
of the ministers of justice or [because of] another aspect that is not
held as sin or punishable that ought to be held as such and punished
or at least impeded. According to the law of God in the forum of
conscience, this cannot be tolerated or allowed before he is punished
and ordered to make restitution. In such a case, the confessor does
not have recourse to another remedy because he is obligated, as was
proven above, to constrain the penitent in the way said. Even before
they may enter into confession, he must make the suitable and sufficient pledge obligating all of his goods before a public notary, giving
power to the ecclesiastical and secular judiciaries so that they may be
able constrain him to make restitution as was said in the first rule.

[56] [Second], or he may make modest and guaranteed deposits
toward [restitution]. Or when all might fail and might be impossible,
make him give the said *juratoria* pledge by legally swearing before a
scribe that within a certain time he will pay what he owes and satisfy
for the harms he did to someone. And in this way the confessor will
fulfill his public duty that God has given to him for the benefit and
the usefulness of his church, and thus he will do what is owed to God.

[57] The suitable or sufficient pledge or firm assurance in accord
with law ought to be given, which means that deposits or pledges
may be given that may be worth the sum he is obligated to restore
or satisfy, as seems to be [derived] from the law *Mandado Titii, &
últi., ff. mandati [de Digesta 17.1.59]; et. 1 [ex]. 4, & adiici, ff. de fidei
commi. lib, [de Digesta 40.5.4] et institu. de rerum divi., & vendite.*[42]

---

42. *Institutions*, in *Digesta of Justinian*, 2.1.41, and *vendite*. [ABP]

[In this manner] the doctors and the glosses noted it in the chapter "Quanquam," already mentioned, *In verbo idonee*,[43] in the chapter "Ad nostram," the 1, *De iure iur.*, *in verbo sufficienti*, in the final chapter "De pigno., in verbo idonee," and in the chapter "Ex publico. de conversio. coniuga."[44]

[58] Thus, applying all that was said to our proposal concerning the restitutions in these Indies, there are two primary types of persons who are obligated to make restitution there, as appears in the aforesaid rules. The first, conquistadors, all those who have been kidnappers and robbers and the most capable in evil and cruelty that never before has ever been and to all the world is already manifest. Concerning such as these, the law has determined, as is said in the chapter "Super eo, de raptoribus," what the confessor must and is obligated to do, even if he might not want to, which is to constrain them to make, not the *juratoria* pledge but rather, as is fitting to know, suitable and sufficient deposits or guarantees or public obligation (as was said in the first and fifth rules and briefly above now is said), and this is proved by the aforementioned texts. And here it is considered that, according to the legal doctors and canonists, the *juratoria* pledge is never enough when each of the others [deposits, guarantees, or public obligation] can be given, and so it is noted in the chapter "Ex parte, de verborum significationibus."[45]

[59] The second [type of persons] obligated to make restitution in the Indies is the encomenderos, and because their debts are many, and the aggrieved, deprived, tyrannized, and afflicted (who are the Indians) are unable to attain justice because of the blindness and perhaps great malice of the temporal ministers of [justice] [by their] not holding as unjust, tyrannical, and iniquitous what is so contrary to natural and divine law and to the law of all the peoples in these nations [which injustice] is committed and always has been committed. And the quantity of what must [be paid] in restitution and satisfaction is very large, and because there is vehement and certain suspicion and juridical presumption that such penitents will never make restitution, the one [reason is] because of the same blindness and even obstinacy

43. *Liber sextus decretalium* of Boniface VIII, in *Decretals of Gregory IX*, bk. 5, title 5, ch. 2, in the gloss on *in verbo indonee*. [ABP]
44. "Ex parte, de verborum significationibus," in *Decretals of Gregory IX*, bk. 2, title 24, ch. 7v; bk. 3, title 21, ch. 8v; *idonee*, bk. 3, title 32, ch. 7. [ABP]
45. *Decretals of Gregory IX*, bk. 5, title 17, ch. 2; bk. 5, title 40, ch. 23. [ABP]

they have; the other is their little fear of God and his condemnation that they feel. The other [is] because they have confessed themselves many times and have left abstaining from telling the truth when they were able to confess themselves, and for other reasons that appear above and more that we omit saying in order to not make a longer process [of this matter]. Therefore, concerning these things, if the confessor wants to do what he ought and to emerge free from this great danger [of insincere confessions], he ought to constrain such a penitent so that he may give the said solemn pledge, as was said in the seventh and eighth rules and following the rest of what is said in this appendix. Because any other way, there will not be some remedy for the tribulations of the dispossessed, oppressed, and afflicted and for the condemnation of the souls of the oppressors, tormentors, and despoilers.[46]

[60] From all that was said they will know, if they might wish to know, [that even] those who consider it harsh that the confessor of the guilty tyrannical penitents in these Indies must require them to make an obligation [at the point of] death or in life to pay restitution for what they robbed, before they might confess; [however], the sums were so great and so difficult to repay as restitution after they have been stolen from others, and these [amounts] were also taken by disproportionate means and obtained by the blood of so many people. [For this reason], the confessors who have not fulfilled or fulfill badly the obligations of their spiritual and public duties are the cause of three great damages, perhaps never rectifiable.

[61] First, during the time that the penitent fails to make restitution, he never makes a sincere confession or does his penitence. And because of this procrastination in making restitution and satisfaction, he passes year after year in mortal sin because of such great burdens and debts. And better to say that they [these penitents] are not procrastinating, but rather with stubborn will they do not want to do this [restitution or satisfaction] until near death. Yet at the end of their days, because some confessor did (what he should have done) and orders him to make restitution, only God knows if he will receive his [free] will [intention] and labor when he can no longer delay what he can offer to him.

46. This indicates that the indigenous peoples would receive justice and that the penitent would do what is just by making restitution and then would be absolved.

[62] Second, the confessor offends and does a great injustice to the dispossessed and robbed and afflicted deserving Indians, since he is judge between them and the penitent, placed there by God as a remedy and light of souls in the church, by not providing for a way that the sentence [that] he gives during the act of confession—where he has all authority—that may have its desired effect such that the aggrieved party, who has less of what pertains to him, may be given equality and a measure of justice. And he who has more, who is the robber and aggravator, may take for himself [what is] for restitution; [as such] what of more he has, he carries with him to hell.

[63] Third, [the confessor] harms himself by not exercising well and justly his spiritual and public office. He is neither the prudent nor the faithful minister of God and of the universal church. From this will result many times the incurring of mortal sin, as Richard [de Mediavilla] says in the 4°, disti. 18, art. 2, q. 5, doing it deliberately or out of *ignorancia iuris affectata* (feigned ignorance of the law) or gross [error], since it is not licit for priests to ignore their duty, as Saint Thomas [says] [*Summa Theologiae*] I–II, 76, 2 ca. And beyond this, [the confessor] is obligated to make restitution and satisfaction for what the penitent should have done for the harms the aggrieved one or aggrieved ones suffer, [and does so] all during the time that the guilty one does not make restitution.[47] Richard holds

47. See the discussion of Ricardus de Mediavilla (Richard Middleton) in paragraph 34 of the translation. The *Digesta of Justinian*, 1.18.6, treats the power of the keys at the hour of pardoning sins. He alludes also to the necessity of the priest possessing the corresponding *discernendi scientia*. He points also to the idea of *ignorantia iuris*, a theme which is treated more fully in Aquinas, *Summa theologica*, 2a–2ae, q. 76, art. 2, c. "Ignorantia vero importat scientiae privationem, dum scilicet alicui deest scientia eorum quae aptus natus est scire." (Ignorance means a lack of knowledge, specifically on the part of those born capable of knowing those matters of which they lack knowledge.)

"Horum autem quaedam aliquis scire tenetur, illa scilicet sine quorum scientia non potest debitum actum recte exercere. Unde omnes tenetur scire communiter ea quae sunt fidei, et universalia juris praecepta; singuli autem ea quae ad eorum statum vel officium spectant." (Some of these matters a person is obliged to know, namely, those in ignorance of which he or she cannot properly perform an obligatory action. All people are accordingly obliged to share a knowledge ["scire communiter"] of what pertains to faith, along with the universal precepts of law; individually, however, we must know what pertains to our status or role in society).

"Manifestum est autem, quod quicumque negligit habere vel facere id quod tenetur habere vel facere, peccat peccato omissionis. Unde propter negligentiam ignorantia eorum quae aliquis scire tenetur, est peccatum; non autem imputatur homini ad

this [position] expressly in the dist. 15 of note 4, [where he asserts] that the harm that comes to the sick person is imputed to the medical doctor as a result of his unskillfulness or negligence, as appears ff. *de offi. presi.*, 1. *illicitas*, § *sicuti medico.* The same thing is said in the glosses, *Ibi de quolibet artifice.* per & *celus*, 1. *si quis fundum*;[48] and per & *Si gemma*, 1. *Item queritur*, ff. *locati.*[49]

[64] The same is [true] for the adviser and judge, who [in carrying out his duties] of sentencing or advising as he ought, [renders a] bad judgement or advice or allows [this] out of ignorance or negligence or imprudence, *ut in* 1. *hoc edicto*, ff. *quod quisquam iuris. Quod turpe est nobili patricio ignorare iura in quibus versatur, ut* ff. *de origi. iur.*, 1. 2., that is, because of unskillfulness or negligence *equiparatur culpe, ut institu.*, ad 1. *aquiliam*, § *imperitia.* All the aforementioned can be proved in the chapter "Si culpa. de iniuriis et damno dato," where it is said, "Si culpa tua datum est damnum vel iniuria irrogata seu aliis irroganitbus opem forte tulisti, aut hec imperitia sive negligentia tua evenerunt, iure super his satisffacere te oportet (hec ignorantia te excusat si scire debuisti ex facto tuo iniuriam verisimiliter posse contingere vel iacturam), and so on." *Haec ibi.*[50] And for our purpose, note what Augustine said in a marvelous sort of way, which is recorded in the *Decretos* (14, questi. 6, chapter. *Si res.*): "Fidentissime (inquit) dixerim, eum qui pro homine ad hoc intervenit ne male ablata restituat, et qui ad se confugientem (quantum honeste postest) ad reddemdum non compellit, socium esse fraudis et criminis. Nam misericordius opem nostram talibus substrahimus, quam impendimus. Hec Augusti."[51] Thus, consider if the confessor ought to fear

---

negligentiam si nesciat ea quae scire non potest." (It is clear, moreover, that whoever neglects to perform or sustain what he or she is obliged to perform or sustain sins by a sin of omission. For this reason, ignorance of matters that one is obliged to know is a sin of negligence, but negligence is not imputed to the person who does not know what he or she cannot know.)

48. From the gloss of the *Digesta of Justinian*, 33.7.12 § Celus. [ABP]

49. *Digesta of Justinian*, 19.2.13 § *gemma.* [ABP]

50. These citations were not found. "If through your fault . . . concerning inflicted suffering and loss," where it is said that, if through your own fault the loss or suffering was inflicted, even if you aided only those who brought it about or if it happened on account of your ignorance or negligence, the law obliges you to make satisfaction, and this ignorance does not excuse you if you ought to have known that suffering or loss could very well have resulted from your actions, and so on.

51. "Augustine Epistola ad Macedonium (it is n° 153) "Illud vero fidentissime dixerim, eum qui pro homine ad hoc intervenit ne male ablata restituat, et qui ad se

being a companion and participant in the crime and sin of the one who robs and destroys his neighbors and [thus has] the obligation to make restitution for what was stolen.

[65] And [concerning] the poor friar who sought to save himself by leaving behind all [that] he might possess in the world (as well as being simpleminded),[52] but was unable to do so, might he go to hell for the sin or [for the] most mortal sins that the men who do not fear God commit and be obliged to make restitution for the pleasure, pomp, and gifts that they sustained and enjoyed with the blood of those they killed and oppressed? It does not seem good advice to not fear and to not be extra careful and to err in so arduous and dangerous a matter.

[66] And with this matter, we conclude, the confessor must also be warned that he is obligated to advise the penitent in this [matter] and in the other case [of his] sin or obligation for restitution; even though [the penitent] may be invincibly ignorant, [the confessor] is to make [the penitent] conscious of it if he is not confessing it, even though he may say that he has confessed to other confessors, and they have not made him conscious of it. [This is imperative] inasmuch as there is no one in the Indies who is invincibly ignorant, since everybody knows about the tyrannies, ravages, cruelties, and robberies that they did. This is proven expressively by Saint Augustine in the book *De penitencia*, dist. 6, cap. 1, where he says, "Caveat spiritualis iudex ut sicut non commisit crimen nequitie, ita non careat munere scientie. O portet ut sciat cognoscere quicquid debet iudicare. Iudiciaria enim potestas hoc postulat, ut quod debet iudicare, discernat. Diligens

---

confugientem, quantum honeste potest, ad restituendum non compellit, socium esse fraudis et criminis. Nam misericordius opem nostram talibus subtrahimus, quam impendimus; non enim opem fert qui ad peccandum adiuvat, ac nos potius subvertit atque opprimit." (I should say with much confidence that he who intervenes on someone's behalf, lest that person should have to restore ill-gotten goods, and who—out of self-interest—does not [as well as he is able to] compel the person to make restitution is an accomplice to the wrong and to the crime. For it is greater mercy to withhold our support from such persons than to give it; one who abets us in sin does not actually help us at all but subverts and oppresses us.) Augustine, *Sancti aurelii augustini hipponensis episcopi*, 2:796. [BLC, *Avisos*]

52. This passage seems to refer to the friar who sought only temporal satisfaction from possessions or his meals (in the *Confesionario*, Las Casas states "no se harta de sopas") or, in colloquial jargon, to a "fraile de misa y olla" (literally "friar of Mass and the kettle," meaning a "simpleminded friar"). *Confesionario*, in *Obras completas*, 10:387.

igitur inquisitor, subtilis investigator sapienter et quasi astute interroget a peccatore quod forsitam ignorat vel verecundia velit occultare. Haec ille."[53] And the gloss, "In verbo investigator, says quod
specialiter in penitente querendum est an hoc vel illud commiserit"
(arg., 43 di., cap. *sit rector*).[54] And the Lord says in Ezekiel, chapter
3, "Fili hominis speculatorem dedi te domui Israel" and, in chapter
33, "si speculator viderit gladium venientem (from the word of God
or from divine precept or from mortal sin or from eternal damnation) et non insonuerit buccina (by declaring the bad state in which
the penitent is in) et populus se non custodierit veneritque gladius
(which is the devil) et tulerit de eis animam, ille quidem in iniquitate
sua captus est, sanguinem autem eius de manu speculatoris requiram.
Hec ibi."[55] Who doubts that when the confessor admits the sinner for

53. "Augustine 'Liber de vera et falsa poenitentia.' Caveat spiritualis judex,
ut sicut non commisit crimen nequitiae, ita non careat munere scientiae. Oportet ut
sciat cognoscere quid debet judicare. Judiciaria, enim potestas hoc postulat, ut quod
debet judicare discernat. Diligens igitur inquisitor, subtilis investigator, sapienter et
quasi astute interroget a peccatore quod forsitan ignoret, vel verecundia velit occultare.
Cognito itaque crimine, marietates eius non dubitet investigare, et locum, et tempus,
et caetera quae supra diximus in exponendo eorum qualitates. Quibus cognitis adsit
benevolus, paratus erigere, et secum onus portare. Habeat dulcedinem in affectione,
pietatem in alterius crimine, discretionem in varietate." (Let the spiritual judge take
care of lacking insight so that he may avoid committing a crime of wickedness, sinning
from lack of knowledge. He should take pains to understand the matter on which he
will pass judgment, for the judicial power requires that one scrutinize what is to be
judged. Let the careful inquirer be a subtle investigator then and wisely and astutely
find out what the sinner might be ignorant of or what he or she might wish to conceal
out of shame. And thus having ascertained the sin, let him not hesitate to investigate
the details, the time, the place, and whatever else pertains to the circumstances as we
have explained above. Knowing these things, let him be benevolent, ready to correct,
and to carry his burden responsibly. Let him show gentleness in his demeanor, solicitude for the sin of the other, and discretion concerning the details.) Augustine, *Liber de
vera et falsa poenitentia*, vol. 40, ch. 20, note 36, p. 1129. [BLC, *Avisos*]
54. *Decretum of Gratian, Treatise on Laws*, dist. 43, c. 1. [ABP]
55. Ez 3:17: "Son of man, I have appointed you a sentinel for the house of Israel.
When you hear a word from my mouth, you shall warn them for me." Ez 33:2–6: "Son
of man, speak to your people and tell them: When I bring the sword against a land,
if the people of that land select one of their number as a sentinel for them, and the
sentinel sees the sword coming against the land, he should blow the trumpet to warn
the people. If they hear the trumpet but do not take the warning and a sword attacks
and kills them, their blood will be on their own heads. They heard the trumpet blast
but ignored the warning; their blood is on them. If they had heeded the warning, they
could have escaped with their lives. If, however, the sentinel sees the sword coming and
does not blow the trumpet, so that the sword attacks and takes someone's life, his life

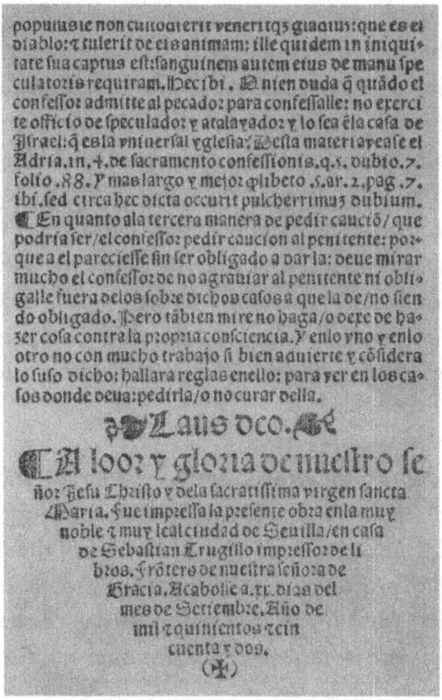
populus se non custodierit venerit qz gladius: que es el diablo: ⁊ tulerit de eis animam: ille quidem in iniquitate sua captus est: sanguinem autem eius de manu speculatoris requiram. Hec ibi. Quien duda q̃ quãdo el confessor admitte al pecador para confessalle: no exercite officio de speculador y atalayador y lo sea ẽla casa de Israel: q̃ es la vniuersal yglesia: Desta materia vease el Adria. in. 4. de sacramento confessionis. q. 5. dubio. 7. folio. 88. Y mas largo y mejor q̃libeto. 5. ar. 2. pag. 7. ibi. sed circa hec dicta occurit pulcherrimuz dubium.
¶ En quanto ala tercera manera de pedir caució / que podria ser / el confessor pedir caucion al penitente: porque a el pareciesse sin ser obligado a darla: deue mirar mucho el confessor de no agrauiar al penitente ni obligalle fuera delos sobre dichos casos a que la de / no siendo obligado. Pero tãbien mire no haga / o dexe de hazer cosa contra la propria consciencia. Y enlo vno y enlo otro no con mucho trabajo si bien aduierte y cõsidera lo suso dicho: hallara reglas enello: para ver en los casos donde deua: pedirla / o no curar della.

Laus deo.

¶ A loor y gloria de nuestro señor Jesu Christo y dela sacratissima virgen sancta Maria. Fue impressa la presente obra enla muy noble ⁊ muy leal ciudad de Seuilla / en casa de Sebastian Trugillo impressor de libros. Frõtero de nuestra señora de Gracia. Acabose a. xx. dias del mes de Settembre. Año de mil ⁊ quinientos ⁊ cincuenta y dos.

FIG. 4 "Laus Deo: El loor y gloria de nuestra fe" (Praise to God, the laud, and glory of our faith) constitutes the ending of Bartolomé de Las Casas's 1552 *Confesionario*. Photograph courtesy of Biblioteca Nacional de Chile, Santiago.

confession, he does not exercise his duty as sentinel and sentry[56] in the house of Israel, that is, the universal church? About this matter, one may consult Adrian's *De sacramento confessionis*, bk. 4, q. 5, dubio 7, folio 88, [or] more thorough and better still, [his] *Quodlibeto*, 5, art. 2, page 7, ibi: *sed circa hec dicta occurit pulcherrimum dubium*.[57]

---

will be taken for his own sin, but I will hold the sentinel responsible for his blood." [BLC, *Avisos*]

56. The Spanish word *atalayador* has various possible translations: sentinel or guard stationed in a watchtower, observer, or investigator.

57. Las Casas does not specify what is treated. Judging from the content and treatment, this seems to be from the work of Adrian VI. Cfr. Hardiani Sexti Pontificus

[67] Regarding the third way of asking for a pledge, the confessor would be able to ask for a pledge from the penitent, since to him [the penitent] it might have seemed, without being obligated to give it, that the confessor is being careful not to aggrieve or obligate him outside of the aforementioned cases to which he is obligated, [that is, those cases to which he] is not obligated. But also he [the confessor] must see to it that [the penitent] does not do or leave undone anything against his own conscience. In either case with great effort, if he [the confessor] carefully notices and considers the aforementioned, he will discover rules about it in order to see the cases wherein he ought to ask for [the pledge] or ought not to prescribe [the pledge].

Praise, laud, and glory to our God and to our Lord Jesus Christ and for the most holy Saint Virgin Mary. The present work was printed in the most noble and very loyal city of Seville, in the house of Sebastián Trujillo, printer of books. Under the protection of Our Lady of Grace, this text was finished the twentieth day of the month of September, the year one thousand five hundred and fifty two.

Maximi, *Quaestiones in quartum sententiarum*. Adrian expounded on the cases of just war and the obligation of restitution, which corresponded to the diverse ways of collaboration, and he indicated what did not correspond to this type of war.

Adorno, Rolena. *The Polemics of Possession in Spanish American Narrative.* New Haven, CT: Yale University Press, 2014.

Adrian VI. *Quaestiones in quartum sententiarum ubi sacramentorum materia exactissime tractatur.* Paris: Chevallonius, 1530.

Alvarez, Jesús H. "Fray Bartolomé de Las Casas, Provincia de Santiago de México." *Ensayos 8 de Cuadernos Dominicanos* (1984): 5–58.

Aquinas, Thomas. *Quaestiones disputatae de veritate.* Edited by R. W. Schmidt. Translated by Robert W. Mulligan and James V. McGlinn. 3 vols. Indianapolis: Hackett Classics, 1994.

———. *Summa theologica.* New York: Benziger Brothers, 1947.

Augustine. *Liber de vera et falsa poenitentia.* In *Patrologiae cursus completus: Series Latina,* edited by Jacques-Paul Migne. Paris: Venit Apud Editorem, 1845.

———. *Sancti Aurelii Augustini hipponensis episcopi Opera omnia.* Vols. 32–46 of *Patrologiæ cursus completus: Series Latina,* edited by Jacques-Paul Migne. Paris: Venit Apud Editorem, 1845.

Baptiste, Victor. *Bartolomé de Las Casas and Thomas More's Utopia: Connections and Similarities.* Culver City, CA: Labyrinth Press, 1990.

Barreda, Jesús Ángel. *Ideología y pastoral misionera en Bartolomé de Las Casas.* Madrid: Institutos Pontificios de Filosofía y Teología, 1981.

Bataillon, Marcel. "The *Clérigo* Casas, Colonist and Colonial Reformer." In Friede and Keen, *Bartolomé de Las Casas,* 353–440.

Beckjord, Sarah H. *Territories of History: Humanism, Rhetoric, and the Historical Imagination.* University Park: Penn State University Press, 2008.

Boer, Wietse de. *The Conquest of the Soul: Confession, Discipline, and Public Order in Counter-Reformation Milan.* Leiden, Netherlands: Brill, 2001.

Borges, Pedro. *Quién era Bartolomé de Las Casas.* Madrid: Ediciones Rialp, 1990.

Boyle, Leonard E. "The Summa Confessorum of John of Freiburg and the Popularization of the Moral Teaching of St. Thomas and of Some of His Contemporaries." In *St. Thomas Aquinas, 1274–1974: Commemorative Studies,* edited by Armand Maurer, 2:245–68. Toronto: Pontifical Institute of Medieval Studies, 1974.

Brooks, Peter. *Troubling Confessions: Speaking Guilt in Law and Literature.* Chicago: University of Chicago Press, 2000.

Brundage, James A. *Medieval Canon Law: The Medieval World.* London: Longman, 1995.

Cantú, Francesca. "Evoluzione e significato della dottrina della restituzione in Bartolomé de Las Casas." *Critica storica* 12, nos. 2–4 (1975): 231–319.

Carrillo Cázares, Alberto. *El debate sobre la guerra chichimeca, 1531–1585: Derecho y política en la Nueva España.* Vol. 1. Zamora, Mexico: El Colegio de Michoacán, 2000.

Castañeda Delgado, Paulino. "Las doctrinas sobre la coacción y el 'idearium' de Las Casas." In Las Casas, *Obras completas*, 2:xxvii.

Catechism of the Catholic Church. Rev. ed. London: Bloomsbury Academic, 2000.

Catholic Study Bible. Edited by Donald Senior and John J. Collins. 2nd ed. New York: Oxford University Press, 2011.

Clayton, Lawrence A. *Bartolomé de Las Casas: A Biography.* Cambridge: Cambridge University Press, 2012.

Coffey, David. *The Sacrament of Reconciliation.* Collegeville, MN: Liturgical Press, 2001.

Consilia et quaestiones. Lyon: Lugduni-Vincentius de Portonarijs Press, 1520.

Cook, Karoline P. "Muslims and *Chichimeca* in New Spain: The Debates over Just War and Slavery." *Anuario de Estudios Americanos* 70, no. 1 (2013): 15–38.

Córdoba, Pedro de. "Carta al rey, del Padre Fray Pedro de Córdoba . . . en 28 de Mayo [1517]." In *Colección de documentos inéditos relativos al descubrimiento, conquista, y organización de las antiguas posesiones españolas de América y oceanía sacados de los archivos del reino y muy especialmente del de Indias*, edited by Joaquín F. Pacheco and Francisco de Cárdenas, 11:221–24. 42 vols. Madrid: Perez/Misericordia, 1869.

"Council of Trent, Session XIV, Chapter IV, on the Most Holy Sacraments of Penance and Extreme Unction." Accessed March 23, 2016. www .thecounciloftrent.com/ch14.htm.

Dallen, James. *The Reconciling Community: The Rite of Penance.* New York: Pueblo Books, 1986.

Daly, Kathleen. "Revisiting the Relationship Between Retributive and Restorative Justice." In *Restorative Justice: From Philosophy to Practice*, edited by Heather Strang and John Braithwaite, 33–54. Aldershot, England: Ashgate/Dartmouth 2000.

Decretals domini of Pope Gregory IX. Edited by Nicolas de Benedictis. Lyon: Lugduni Press, 1505.

Decretals of Gregory IX. Friedberg edition. Leipzig, 1879–81.

Decretum of Gratian. Friedberg edition. Leipzig, 1879–81.

De Heredia, Vicente Beltrán. *Cartulario de la universidad de Salamanca (1218–1600).* 5 vols. Salamanca: Ediciones Universidad Salamanca, 1970–72.

Didache. Translated by Charles H. Hoole. Christian Apologetics and Research Ministry. Accessed April 6, 2016. https://carm.org/didache.

Digesta of Justinian. 2 vols. Berlin: Apud Weidmannos, 1870.

Dutto, Anthony A. *The Life of Bartolomé de Las Casas and the First Leaves of American Ecclesiastical History*. St. Louis: Herder, 1902. Reprint, London: Forgotten Books, 2013.

Dutton, Richard, Alison Gail Findlay, and Richard Wilson. *Theatre and Religion: Lancastrian Shakespeare*. New York: Manchester University Press, 2003.

Espinel, José Luis. *San Esteban de Salamanca: Historia y guía (siglos XIII–XX)*. Salamanca: Editorial San Esteban, 1995.

Fabié, Antonio María. *Vida y escritos de fray Bartolomé de Las Casas*. 2 vols. Madrid: Ginesta, 1879.

Favazza, Joseph A. *The Order of Penitents: Historical Roots and Pastoral Future*. Collegeville, MN: Liturgical Press, 1988.

Fernández Rodríguez, Pedro. *Los dominicos en el contexto de la primera evangelización de México, 1526–1550*. Salamanca: Editorial San Esteban, 1994.

Floyd, Shawn, ed. "Thomas Aquinas: Moral Philosophy." *Internet Encyclopedia of Philosophy*. Accessed March 31, 2016. www.iep.utm.edu/aq-moral/.

Frades Gaspar, Eduardo. *El uso de la Biblia en los escritos de Fray Bartolomé de Las Casas*. Caracas: Instituto Universitario Seminario Interdiocesano, 1992.

Friede, Juan. "Las Casas and Indigenism." In Friede and Keen, *Bartolomé de Las Casas*, 127–234.

Friede, Juan, and Benjamin Keen, eds. *Bartolomé de Las Casas in History: Toward an Understanding of the Man and His Work*. DeKalb: Northern Illinois University Press, 1971.

Galmés, Lorenzo, O.P. "Nota introductoria." In Las Casas, *Obras completas*, 10:365.

García Icazbalceta, Joaquín. *Colección de documentos para la historia de México*. 2 vols. Mexico City: Librería de J. M. Andrade/Antigua Librería, 1858–66.

García-Morato-Soto, Juan Ramón. "La necesidad de la confesión de los pecados en Domingo de Soto." *Sacra Theologia* 15 (1988): 225–91.

García-Serrano, Francisco. *Preachers of the City: The Expansion of the Dominican Order in Castile (1217–1348)*. New Orleans: University Press of South, 1997.

Gil, Fernando. "Las Juntas Eclesiásticas durante el episcopado de Fray Juan de Zumárraga (1528–1548): Algunas precisiones históricas." *Teología: Revista de la Facultad de Teología de la Pontificia Universidad Católica Argentina*, no. 54 (1989): 7–34.

Giménez Fernández, Manuel. *Bartolomé de Las Casas: Capellán de S. M. Carlos I, poblador de Cumaná, 1517–1523*. 2 vols. Madrid: Consejo Superior de Investigaciones Científicas, 1984.

————. *Bartolomé de Las Casas: Delegado de Cisneros para la Reformación de Las Indias, 1516–1517.* Madrid: Consejo Superior de Investigaciones Científicas, 1984.

————. "Fray Bartolomé de Las Casas: A Biographical Sketch." In Friede and Keen, *Bartolomé de Las Casas,* 67–126.

Goering, Joseph. "The Internal Forum and the Literature of Penance and Confession." *Traditio* 59, no. 1 (2004): 175–227.

Gratian. *The Treatise on Laws (Decretum DD. 1–20) with the Ordinary Gloss.* Translated by Augustine Thompson and James Gordley. Washington, DC: Catholic University of America Press, 1993.

Gutiérrez, Antonio Rodríguez. "El 'Confesionario' de Bartolomé de Las Casas." *Ciencia Tomista* 102, no. 33 (1975): 249–78.

Gutiérrez, Gustavo. *Las Casas: In Search of the Poor of Jesus Christ.* Translated by Robert R. Barr. Maryknoll, NY: Orbis Books, 1993.

Halsall, Paul, ed. "Medieval Sourcebook: The Seven Sacraments; Catholic Doctrinal Documents: Decree for the Armenians Council of Florence 1439." *Internet Medieval Source Book.* Fordham University. Last modified November 4, 2011. http://sourcebooks.fordham.edu/source /1438sacraments.asp.

————. "Medieval Sourcebook: Twelfth Ecumenical Council; Lateran IV 1215: Canon 21." *Internet Medieval Source Book.* Fordham University. Accessed December 28, 2015. https://sourcebooks.fordham.edu/basis /lateran4.asp.

Hanke, Lewis. *All Mankind Is One: A Study of the Disputation Between Bartolomé de Las Casas and Juan Ginés de Sepúlveda in 1550 on the Intellectual and Religious Capacity of the American Indians.* De Kalb: Northern Illinois University Press, 1974.

————. *The Spanish Struggle for Justice in the Conquest of America.* Dallas: Southern Methodist University Press, 2002.

Hanke, Lewis, and Manuel Giménez Fernández. *Bartolomé de Las Casas, 1474–1566: Bibliografía crítica y cuerpo de materiales para el estudio de su vida, actuación y polémica que suscitaron durante cuatro siglos.* Santiago, Chile: Fondo Histórico, 1954.

Harrison, Regina. *Sin and Confession in Colonial Peru: Spanish-Quechua Penitential Texts, 1560–1650.* Austin: University of Texas Press, 2014.

Hartmann, Wilfried, and Kenneth Pennington, eds. *The History of Canon Law in the Classical Period, 1140–1234: From Gratian to the Decretals of Pope Gregory IX.* Washington, DC: Catholic University of America Press, 2008.

Hernández Franco, Juan. *Cultura y limpieza de sangre en la España moderna: Puritate sanguinis.* Murcia, Spain: Editorial Universidad de Murcia, 1997.

Hill, Jonathan. *Faith in the Age of Reason: The Enlightenment from Galileo to Kant.* Oxford: Lion Books, 2004.

Iglesias Ortega, Luis. *Bartolomé de Las Casas: Cuarenta y cuatro años infinitos.* Seville: Fundación José Lara, 2007.

Johnson, James Turner. *Ideology, Reason, and the Limitation of War: Religious and Secular Concepts, 1200–1740*. Princeton: Princeton University Press, 2015.

———. *Just War Tradition and the Restraint of War: A Moral and Historical Inquiry*. Princeton: Princeton University Press, 2014.

Kaplan, Gregory B. "The Inception of *Limpieza de Sangre* (Purity of Blood) and Its Impact in Medieval and Golden Age Spain." In *Marginal Voices: Studies in Converso Literature of Medieval and Golden Age Spain*, edited by Amy Aronson-Friedman and Gregory B. Kaplan, 19–41. Leiden, Netherlands: Brill, 2012.

Kirby, Peter, ed. "Ignatius of Antioch." *Early Christian Writings*. April 6, 2016. www.earlychristianwritings.com/ignatius.html.

Las Casas, Fray Bartolomé de. *Bartolomé de Las Casas: The Only Way.* Edited with an introduction by Helen Rand Parish. Translated by Francis Patrick Sullivan. Mahwah, NJ: Paulist Press, 1992.

———. *Brevísima relación de la destruición de las Indias*. Edited by Isacio Pérez Fernández. Madrid: Editorial Tecnos, 1992.

———. *Historia de las Indias*. Edited by Agustín Millares Carlo. 3 vols. Mexico City: Fondo de Cultura Económica, 1951.

———. *In Defense of the Indians: The Defense of the Most Reverend Lord, Don Fray Bartolomé de Las Casas, of the Order of Preachers, Late Bishop of Chiapa, Against the Persecutors and Slanderers of the Peoples of the New World Discovered Across the Seas*. Translated by Stafford Poole. DeKalb: Northern Illinois University Press, 1974.

———. *Las Casas on Columbus: Background and the Second and Fourth Voyages*. Edited by Anthony Pagden. Translated by Nigel Griffin. Turnhout, Belgium: Brepols, 1999.

———. *Obras completas*. Edited by Paulino Castañeda Delgado. 14 vols. Madrid: Alianza, 1989–92.

———. *Obras escogidas*. Edited by Juan Pérez de Tudela. 5 vols. Madrid: Atlas, 1957–58.

———. *Witness: Writings of Bartolomé de Las Casas*. Edited and translated by George Sanderlin. New York: Knopf, 1971.

Lea, Henry Charles. *Confession and Absolution*. Philadelphia: Lea Brothers, 1896.

———. *A History of Auricular Confession and Indulgences in the Latin Church*. 3 vols. Philadelphia: Lea Brothers, 1896.

Lippy, Charles H., Robert Choquette, and Stafford Poole. *Christianity Comes to the Americas, 1492–1776*. New York: Paragon House, 1992.

Lockhart, James. *The Men of Cajamarca: A Social and Biographical Study of the First Conquerors of Peru*. 1972. Austin: University of Texas Press, 2013.

———. *Spanish Peru: 1532–1560; A Social History*. 2nd ed. Madison: University of Wisconsin Press, 1994.

Losada, Angel. "The Controversy Between Sepulveda and Las Casas in the Junta de Valladolid." In Friede and Keen, *Bartolomé de Las Casas*, 279–308.

Lupher, David A. *Romans in a New World: Classical Models in Sixteenth-Century Spanish America.* Ann Arbor: University of Michigan Press, 2006.

MacNutt, Francis Augustus. *Bartholomew de Las Casas: His Life, His Apostolate, and His Writings.* Cleveland: Clark, 1909.

Mediavilla, Ricardus de. *Super quarto sententiarum.* Lyon: Clein, 1504.

Mulchahey, M. Michèle. *"First the Bow Is Bent in Study. . . .": Dominican Education Before 1350.* Toronto: Pontifical Institute for Medieval Studies, 1998.

Orique, David Thomas. "A Comparison of the Voices of the Spanish Bartolomé de Las Casas and the Portuguese Fernão Oliveira on Just War and Slavery." *E-journal of Portuguese History* 12, no. 1 (2014): 87–118.

————. "New Discoveries About an Old Manuscript: The Date, Place of Origin, and Role of the *Parecer de Fray Bartolomé de Las Casas* in the Making of the New Laws of the Indies." *Colonial Latin American Historical Review* 15, no. 4 (2010): 419–41.

————. "To Heaven or Hell: An Introduction to the Soteriology of Bartolomé de Las Casas." *Bulletin of Spanish Studies* 93, no. 9 (2016): 1495–526.

————. "The Unheard Voice of Law in Bartolomé de Las Casas's *Brevísima relación de la destruición de las Indias.*" PhD diss., University of Oregon, 2011.

Owensby, Brian P. "The Theater of Conscience in the 'Living Law' of the Indies." In *New Horizons in Spanish Colonial Law: Contributions to Transnational Early Modern Legal History*, edited by Thomas Duve and Heikki Pihlajamaki, 125–49. Frankfurt am Main: Max Planck Institute for European Legal History, 2015.

Parish, Helen Rand, and Harold Weidman. *Las Casas en México: Historia y obra desconocidas.* Mexico City: Fondo de Cultura Económica, 1992.

Paz, Matías de. "Del dominio de los reyes de España sobre los Indios." In *De las islas del mar Océano*, by Juan López de Palacios, translated by Agustín Millares Carlo, 213–318. Mexico City: Fondo de Cultura Económica, 1963.

Peñafort, Raymond of. *Summa de paenitentia.* Edited by Xaverio Ochoa and Aloisio Díez. Tomus B. Column 277. Rome: Commentarium pro Religiosis, 1975–78.

Pennington, Kenneth. *Popes, Canonists, and Texts, 1150–1550.* Aldershot, England: Variorum, 1993.

————. "A Short History of Canon Law from Apostolic Times to 1917." Catholic University of America. Accessed July 2, 2017. http://legalhistorysources.com/Canon%20Law/PenningtonShortHistoryCanonLaw.pdf.

Pérez Fernández, Isacio. *Bartolomé de Las Casas, viajero por dos mundos: Su figura, su Biografía sincera, su personalidad.* Cuzco, Peru: Centro de Estudios Regionales Andinos "Bartolomé de Las Casas," 1998.

————. *Cronología documentada de los viajes, estancias, y actuaciones de Fray Bartolomé de Las Casas.* Bayamón, Puerto Rico: Centro de Estudios de los Dominicos del Caribe, 1984.

————. *El derecho Hispano-Indiano: Dinámica social de su proceso histórico constituyente.* Salamanca: Editorial San Esteban, 2001.

————. *Fray Toribio Motolinía, O.F.M., frente a Fray Bartolomé de Las Casas, O.P.: Estudio y edición crítica de la carta de Motolinía al emperador (Tlaxcala, a 2 de enero de 1555).* Salamanca: Editorial San Esteban, 1989.

————. *Inventario documentado de los escritos de Fray Bartolomé de Las Casas.* Edited by Helen Rand Parish. Bayamón, Puerto Rico: Centro de Estudios de los Dominicos del Caribe, 1981.

Phelan, John Leddy. "The Apologetic History of Fray Bartolomé de Las Casas." *Hispanic American Historical Review* 49, no. 1 (1969): 94–99.

————. *The Millennial Kingdom of the Franciscans in the New World: A Study of the Writings of Gerónimo de Mendieta (1525–1604).* Berkeley: University of California Press, 1956.

Picón-Salas, Mariano. *A Cultural History of Spanish America, from Conquest to Independence.* Berkeley: University of California Press, 1962.

Pinelo, Antonio de León. *Epitome de la bibliotheca oriental i occidental, náutica i geográfica.* Madrid: González, 1629.

Platt, Rutherford H., Jr., ed. "The Shepherd of Hermas." In *The Lost Books of the Bible and the Forgotten Books of Eden,* 197–211. Cleveland: World, 1926.

Remesal, Antonio de. *Historia general de las Indias Occidentales y particular de la gobernación de Chiapa y Guatemala. . . .* 3rd ed. 4 vols. Guatemala: Editorial "José de Pineda Ibarra," 1966.

Restall, Matthew. *Seven Myths of the Spanish Conquest.* Oxford: Oxford University Press, 2004.

Rivera-Pagán, Luis N. *A Violent Evangelization: The Political and Religious Conquest of the Americas.* Louisville, KY: Westminster/John Knox Press, 1992.

Roa-de-la-Carrera, Cristián Andrés. *Histories of Infamy: Francisco López de Gómara and the Ethics of Spanish Imperialism.* Boulder: University Press of Colorado, 2005.

Root, Jerry. *Space to Speke: The Confessional Subject in Medieval Literature.* New York: Lang, 1997.

Rouillard, Philippe. *Historia de la penitencia desde los orígenes a nuestros días.* Translated by José Luis Arriaga. Paris: Éditions de Cerf, 1999.

Russell, Frederick H. *The Just War in the Middle Ages.* Cambridge: Cambridge University Press, 1975.

Sáenz de Santa María, Carmelo. *El licenciado don Francisco Marroquín, primer obispo de Guatemala, 1499–1563.* Madrid: Ediciones Cultura Hispánica, 1964.

Sauer, Carl Ortwin. *Land and Life: A Selection from the Writings of Carl Ortwin.* Berkeley: University of California Press, 1969.

Simpson, Lesley Byrd. *The Encomienda in New Spain: The Beginning of Spanish Mexico*. Berkeley: University of California Press, 1982.

Tanner, Norman P., ed. and trans. "Ecumenical Council of Florence (1438–1445): Session 8; 22 November 1439 [Bull of Union with the Armenians]." Eternal Word Television Network. Accessed December 28, 2015. www.ewtn.com/library/councils/Florence.htm#3.

Tentler, Thomas N. "The Summa for Confessors as an Instrument of Social Control." In *The Pursuit of Holiness in Late Medieval and Renaissance Religion*, edited by Charles Trinkaus and Heiko Oberman, 103–26. Leiden, Netherlands: Brill, 1974.

Tibesar, A. "Documents: Instructions for the Confessors of *Conquistadores* Issued by the Archbishop of Lima in 1560." *Americas* 3, no. 4 (1947): 514–34.

Tierney, Brian. *The Idea of Natural Rights: Studies on Natural Rights, Natural Law, and Church Law, 1150–1625*. Atlanta, GA: Scholars Press, 1997.

Urton, Gary. "Sin, Confession, and the Arts of Book- and Cord-Keeping: An Intercontinental and Transcultural Exploration of Accounting and Governmentality." *Comparative Studies in Society and History* 51, no. 4 (2009): 801–31. https://doi:10.1017/S0010417509990144.

Vera, Fortino Hipólito. *Compendio histórico del Concilio III Mexicano, o índices de los tres tomos de la colección del mismo concilio*. Vol. 2. Amecameca, Mexico: Imprenta del Colegio Católico, 1879.

Vickery, Paul S. *Bartolomé de Las Casas: Great Prophet of the Americas*. Mahwah, NJ: Paulist Press, 2006.

Wagner, Henry Raup, and Helen Rand Parish. *The Life and Writings of Bartolomé de Las Casas*. Albuquerque: University of New Mexico Press, 1967.

Walz, A. "Si. Raymundi de Penyafort auctoritas in re poenitentiali." *Angelicum* 12 (1935): 346–96.

la gobernación de las Indias (New Laws, 1542)

Laws of Burgos, 10n14

Leyes y ordenanzas nuevas para la gobernación de las Indias (New Laws, 1542), 24–26, 28
- auditor sent to enforce, 28, 30
- Charles V's abrogation of key provisions of, 28, 30n71, 35
- controversy generated by, 34
- enforcement of
  - Crown efforts to bolster, 28, 30, 30n71
  - Las Casas's recommendations on, 25
- and indigenous rights, 25
- Las Casas's efforts to enforce in Chiapa, 38, 39
- Las Casas's influence on, 24, 25–26
- mendicant friars' junta of 1546 on, 38
- protections for indigenous people in, 24–25
- provisions of, 24–25
- repartimiento system and, 75n3
- Spanish colonists' resistance to, 26–30, 39

Loaysa, García, 43n32
Loaysa, Gerónimo de, 69
Lombard, Peter, 45

MacNutt, Francis, 15
Maldonado, Alonso de, 28, 41–42
Mapa portolano (Ribero), 19
Marroquín, Francisco (bishop of Guatemala)
- complaints about Las Casas's Doce reglas, 41–42
- invitation to Las Casas and brethren, 18
- and Las Casas mission to Spain, 21, 22–23n52
- parting of ways with Las Casas, 26n64

Mayno, Jasón de, 98
"Memorial de remedios" [1542] (Las Casas), 23
"Memorial de remedios para las Indias" [1516] (Las Casas), 9–11

mendicant friars' junta of 1546
- denial of absolution to slave owners, 38
- directives issued by, 37–38
- Las Casas's arrangement of, 30, 37
- Las Casas's influence in, 37

limited information on, 33n1
and writing of Doce reglas para confesores, 33

Mendoza, Antonio de
- attacks on Las Casas's Doce reglas, 41–42, 42n28
- and dispute over clerical immunity, 34
- and friars' junta following synod of 1546, 37, 37n11
- and Mexican ecclesiastical junta of 1539, 22
- and Mexican ecclesiastical synod of 1546, 34–35
- opposition to New Laws, 22n50, 34
- work with Las Casas, 22

merchants
- Confesionario on
  - crimes of, 37–38, 56, 90
  - good faith defense as unavailable to, 77, 90–91
  - restitution required of, 60, 61, 90–91
  - rules pertaining to, 54, 76
- Doce reglas on crimes of, 41

Mexico
- cabildo, and Las Casas's Doce reglas, 41
- ecclesiastical junta (1536), actae, Las Casas's influence on, 20–21
- ecclesiastical junta (1539), Las Casas at, 22
- Las Casas's travel in, 18–20, 21–22
- See also ecclesiastical synod (Mexico City, 1546)

Minaya, Bernardino de, 18
miners, Confesionario on
- crimes of, 57–58
- restitution required from, 88

Mixtón War (1540-1542), 38n12
Montesinos, Antón de, 5n1, 7–8, 9
Morales, Francisco de, 70
Motolinía, Toribio, 41, 42n28

natural law
- Spanish conquest as violation of, 59, 86
- support in, for Las Casas's denial of Sacrament of Confession to abusers of indigenous people, 65–66, 93–101

New Laws. See Leyes y ordenanzas nuevas para la gobernación de las Indias (New Laws, 1542)

ranchers, *Confesionario* on
crimes of, 57–58
restitution required from, 88
Raymond of Peñafort, 93n24, 94–95n32
Remesal, Antonio de, 33n1, 38–39n14
Rentería, Pedro de la, 9
repartimiento system
definition of, 6n3, 75n3
Las Casas's demand for end of, 23–24
Las Casas's involvement in, 5–6
New Laws and, 75n3
persons involved in, as subject to *Doce reglas*, 75
"Representación al emperador Carlos V" (Las Casas), 24
restitution/restoration for indigenous people
arguments for, in Las Casas's Sevillian Cycle, 48
canon law requirement for, Las Casas on, 11, 12, 24
in cases of insufficient funds, 65, 85, 86–87, 88
in cases where restitution is impossible, 63–64, 80–81, 85
confessor's creation of public list of, 80–81
determining amount of, 59–61
Dominicans' calls for, 12
failure to obtain
as crime against injured indigenous people, 103
as crime against sinner allowed to continue in sin, 102
as self-harm by confessor failing in duty to God, 103–5
full, necessity of, 59–60, 61, 63, 76–77, 79–80, 81–82
Las Casas on four proofs of need for, 17
Las Casas's demand for, 1, 2, 8, 11, 16, 41
civil authorities' push-back against, 16
Las Casas's increasing focus on, 15–17
Las Casas's return of his *encomienda*, 8
and Las Casas's *Sobre . . . los Indios que se han hecho en ellas esclavos*, 48, 48n49
Las Casas's teachings on, 20
mandated hardship equal to the poverty caused, 84

as medicine rather than punishment, 67, 93–94
Mexican ecclesiastical junta of 1536 *actae* on, 21
Mexican ecclesiastical synod of 1546 resolution on, 35–36, 37
papal decree on, 21
principle of amicable compensation and, Las Casas on, 11, 12
sources cited to support, 64–66, 82–83, 89, 89n20, 91–107
See also pledge demanded from penitents
Ribero, Diego, 19
Richard de Mediavilla, 89, 89n20, 103–4
Rogel, Juan, 28, 30

sacramento confessionis, De (Adrian), 107
Sacrament of Penance and Reconciliation
denial to Las Casas, 5
reasons for, 5–6
spiritual awakening prompted by, 6–7
as forum of conscience, 38n13
Las Casas's denial to abusers of indigenous people, 1–2, 16, 27–28
Adición to *Confesionario* as justification of, 41, 42, 75, 91
and clerical immunity, need for, 39–40
legally-binding pledge required to lift, 1, 16, 41
mendicant friars' junta of 1546 on, 38
Mexican ecclesiastical synod of 1546's call for restitution and, 36–37
Mexican ecclesiastical synod of 1546's rejection of tactic, 35
practical necessity of, to force contrition and restitution, 101–2
some Dominican's concerns about, 41, 42, 74–75, 91
sources cited to support, 64–66, 64n22, 82–83, 89, 89n20, 91–107
Spanish colonists' push-back against, 16, 28
spiritual consequences of failing to receive, 1–2
Sánchez Coello, Alonso, 6

latin american originals

Titles in Print